# THE
# 60
# SECOND
# SALE

**AVOID BURNOUT, SAVE TIME, AND BECOME
A MEMBER OF THE SALES ELITE**

# ALINE BENDER

# TABLE OF CONTENTS

# FOREWORD

A LINE BENDER AND I became friends in 2006. We hit it off instantly mainly because we were, and are, very similar when it comes to our personal growth and work ethics. I can recall the moment that I knew I could count on Aline's friendship and support. It was in 2006, I was in Florida about to film live on the Home Shopping Network set to sell my first invention: The CreaClip. I needed to know how many teeth were in the comb of my clip. But I didn't have the time to count them. I reached for my phone and called Aline. Sure enough, she picked up the phone even though it was 6:00 am her time in Hawaii. I asked if she would do the tedious job of being my counter. And without any hesitation, she said "ok I'll call you right back." Within less than 5 minutes, she called me back with the information I needed.

Since then, our friendship and co-mentorship grew and continues to thrive. It is my deepest honor to share with you how blessed we are that Aline Bender is sharing her sales method with the world. If you are unsure of her capability to assist you in increasing your sales performance, let me assure you there is no one better.

Once again, Aline came to my need right before I was about to film for a pitch on Shark Tank. I had a feeling that my sales numbers were not intact and that my sales pitch delivery required adjustments. I mean, this pitch was for the infamous investors on Shark Tank! Aline coached me by re-arranging the way I presented my sales numbers and the verbiage I used for my sales pitch. By the time we completed our coaching sessions, I was confident and more than ready to face the Sharks. When the moment arrived at the Tank, I was able to answer all of the questions from my potential investors and let them see the value of investing in me and in CreaProducts. Needless to say, I got a deal!

I am certain that the sales method and sales communication laid out in this book will give you the guidance you need. Take advantage of the power-packed content and proven sales techniques that are readily available for you to learn. I am grateful that I have learned and continue do so from Aline's sales expertise to assist me in my negotiations and in growing my company's sales production.

~ *Mai Lieu*
  CEO CreaProducts
  Shark Tank Contestant Winner
  Author of *Take The Next Step*

# ACKNOWLEDGEMENTS

I HAVE JOKED THAT THIS book was 5 years in the making. In reality, over the past 5 years I've juggled writing this book, getting married, moving to San Diego, CA, and building a mortgage business with my husband.

My daughter Helena has been my biggest inspiration. She drives me to fulfill my dreams and make them a reality. If I expect her to live her life to the fullest, then I must also be held accountable and do the same. Thank you, pumpkin, for letting me practice my sales presentation with you and for believing in me.

The long-awaited release of this book is mainly due to reminders from my husband and my friends Jessica Zeller, Mai Lieu, Sumoha Jani, and Sam King. They kept telling me that I needed to complete it, so that others could benefit from its content. Their words constantly pushed me because I knew that I had to share what I was so fortunate enough to have learned from others.

Without the support of those that were gracious enough to give me valuable lessons, concepts, techniques, and guidance, I wouldn't have accelerated my sales success at the pace I have. Thank you to my editors Tom S. Johnson and Erica Bender, they have been patient and made my writing shine. Likewise, I have much gratitude for my mentors: Darrin Moreman, Terrence Limebrook, Richard Green, Don Nahaku, Dr. John Demartini, Má, and Papa.

# INTRODUCTION

*"When the student is ready, the teacher will appear."*
~ Variously attributed to followers of Buddha,
Zen, Confucius, and Theosophy

●————————————————●

**M**ANY PEOPLE HAVE A defining moment in their childhoods that changes their lives forever. It may have been their parents' divorce, a death in the family, a move across the country, or the loss of their first love. For me, this life-changing moment occurred at the age of ten—when I embarked on a journey halfway across the globe, with only my thirteen-year-old brother to accompany me.

In Paris, France, Charles De Gaulle Airport was filled with the noise of flight announcements and people chatting. As we stood in the Air France check-in line, my father placed a wearable pouch around each of our necks, and he warned us to not take them off for any reason. At the time, I didn't understand the value of the pouches, but they contained our airline tickets, connection information, and luggage tags.

Papa reminded us that we were going to meet our relatives in the United States. He stressed that my brother was in charge, and clarified that our relatives would be waiting for us as soon as we landed in Houston, TX. I felt an intense mixture of excitement and nervousness, as we had never been on a plane without Papa. My brother and I didn't understand how long our trip to the United States would last, and we'd never met these relatives before.

We made it to Houston safe and sound (and well-caffein-ated, due to limitless sodas). As promised, our relatives were excitedly waiting by our arrival gate. I later found out that they were my stepmother, stepbrother, and three stepsisters.

My father and stepmother were married in a private cer-emony the year prior to our trip to the US, but my brother and I didn't know about it. This news was a welcome sur-prise, as our biological mother had been absent throughout much of our childhood. I had yearned for a mother and more siblings for many years, so it was a dream come true. Reflecting on it now, I am amazed at how my stepmother moved mountains and acquired the means to immigrate my brother, father, and me from France to the US.

## THE LANGUAGE BARRIER

This "Coming to America" experience was the first event that shaped my understanding of effective communication.

Now that I had the extended family of my dreams, I had to face the challenges that came along with such a massive life change. The first major problem that I encountered was language; my brother and I only spoke French, while my stepfamily spoke Vietnamese and English. Even though my brother and I are Vietnamese and were born in Vietnam, we didn't speak the language. We had immigrated to France with our father as toddlers, so French was our first language. Now that we were in Houston, the language barrier extended from our family into our new school, so communicating with teachers and fellow classmates (and everyone else we encountered) was also a huge hurdle.

Papa had to stay back in France for an entire year, and my stepmother didn't speak English well herself. Therefore, my brother and I were on our own to learn a new language in a new country.

We started school a few weeks after arriving in the US, which only compounded our feeling that we were aliens that only spoke French. Unfortunately, there was no one to teach us the basics: my school did not have an English as a Second Language (ESL) class for non-English speakers like us. We were thrown into the deep-end of mainstream classes. It was a "sink or swim" situation, and my brother and I were determined to swim.

On my own in my 4th grade class, my teacher didn't know what to do with me. We couldn't even speak to each other; we could only point and nod our heads. She tried her best to include me in the day's lessons, smiling and gesturing like a mime. I would steadily gaze at her, deeply concentrating and trying to make any sense of her charade.

One morning, we were working on spelling. One at a time, my teacher gave my classmates words to spell and asked them to go to the chalkboard and write them out. They were words like "achieve," "competition," and "knowledge."

She wanted to build my confidence, so she called me to the front of the class, handed me a piece of chalk, and nodded encouragingly. Then she asked me to write the simplest word she could think of on the board. "The," she said, slowly enunciating the word and flashing a beaming smile.

Urging me forward, she pointed at the chalk in my hand, then at the chalkboard. I was thrilled. This was easy! I finally had a chance to prove that I wasn't just a strange, quiet import from Europe. I confidently stepped forward, reached up to the board, and started to write. I can still recall the sound of the chalk as it met the board.

With the tip of my tongue pressed between my lips, I happily wrote what I believed I had heard my teacher ask me to spell: "de." (That's the French word for "from"). Childish laughter burst out behind me. As I turned around, my confidence shattered. Half the class were shocked and concerned, so they shouted, "Oooh!" The other half were laughing as they pointed their fingers at me: "This girl can't even spell 'the.'" My teacher looked frustrated and motioned for me to return to my desk. My face burned with humiliation.

Within a few weeks, I grew tired of not being able to communicate with my teacher, classmates, and new family. It was frustrating, as I was eager to form new friendships and build relationships with my newfound family. My teacher gave me the same assignments she gave the rest of the class. Therefore, she returned every one of my assignments with a big fat "F."

## NEW STRATEGIES

Without giving up hope, I tried to create strategies that would help me avoid the depths of despair. I soon realized that if I went up to my teacher's desk and pointed to a white notepad with printed words on it, she would allow me to rip a sheet from the pad and take it to a building filled with books.

One of the first things I learned when I arrived in this building was that it was called a school library. It became my real classroom; it's where I taught myself everything I needed to know. It was my workspace, my playground, my haven, and the birthplace of my self-development. Every day in the main classroom, I pointed to the pad of permission slips to go to the library. Grateful that she didn't have to cater to me, the teacher gladly obliged. And off I went, eager and excited to learn English.

I spent my time in the kindergarten reading section as I taught myself to read—sitting on a tiny chair with my knees up to my chin and looking at brightly colored picture books. When I saw an image of "un cochon" with its snout in the mud, I would carefully sound out the word in the text: "P...I...G." For many hours, I practiced reading and spelling, connecting the pictures to their names, and sounding out the words.

Another exciting discovery came in the form of a show that appeared on television every day after school. I would rush home to watch a huge yellow bird and other puppets on *Sesame Street*. A vampire puppet named "The Count" became my math teacher. He helped me pronounce the English numbers with his "Ahhhh a-One... and ahhhh a-Two!" The rest of the *Sesame Street* cast became my tutors.

Within five months of reading every day in the school's library and learning from my puppet tutors, I was speaking, writing, and reading English. To improve my English language skills further, I participated in a school fundraiser. I went door-to-door, asking people to buy beef jerky. After eating a third of my stash and selling the rest, I became more confident in my English communication skills.

I also signed up for the school choir. The first song we learned was Whitney Houston's "The Greatest Love of All," but I didn't realize that singing in English was more difficult than speaking. In order to save nearby students from my tuneless mumblings, I generally just lip-synced.

During my first year in the US, I received straight Ds and Fs. While embarrassing, it didn't stop me from achieving my goal of fluently communicating in English. Between my thirst for learning and my commitment to succeed, it wasn't long before I was excelling in school. In fact, I soon started receiving straight A's, which astounded my teachers.

By age 11, Papa had come to the US and my family moved from Houston to Southern California. When we moved to California, I started going to a school that offered ESL, but by then I no longer needed English tutors.

## DETERMINING OUR OWN POTENTIAL

Adverse life circumstances alone do not determine our potential for achievement. Rather, we determine it ourselves with our mindset, choices, discipline, and action.

In October 2005, I found myself going through a divorce. I was a newly-single mother of a two-year-old girl and living in one of the most expensive states in the country: Hawaii. I desperately needed a well-paying job. I knew that I wanted to be in sales, but didn't want to be in just any position. Rather, I wanted to use my talent for communication and my prowess for understanding people's needs and desires. Then I could assist them in making one of the biggest decisions of their lives. I didn't just want to sell houses; I wanted to sell *homes.*

Being a realtor was the perfect profession for me, and I was excited to be offered a position with a prestigious real estate company. However, at the new-hire orientation, we were told that we each needed to pay $3,500 dollars to create a personal marketing campaign. I literally had $50 in my bank account, so I had to turn that position down.

Undeterred, I pursued a sales position with Fairfield Resorts (now called Wyndham Vacation Resorts or WVO). After six months of persistently calling the recruiter and asking for an opportunity to be a sales representative, I was finally hired. My persistence paid off.

I remember walking from an outdoor parking lot to start my first day of work. I stopped for a moment, experienced a true feeling of calm, and heard myself say: "I will be in this position for five years." Looking back on that moment, I don't know where that thought came from—because prior to taking that position, I didn't stay in any job for more than two years. I had no idea that the success rate in the vacation ownership industry was less than 2% during the first year, and even less thereafter.

Let me define what I consider to be success in the vacation ownership industry:

1. Consistently earning over $100,000 per year in commission.
2. Staying employed long enough to be invited to the company's holiday party.

The local inside joke was that Senior Sales Representatives didn't learn the rookies' names until they'd made it to the holiday party. I mentally prepared myself and set a goal to be at that party. I knew I could make it.

On my first day in the office, I tried to look my best, although the only new professional-looking shoes I could afford set me back a whopping $13. With my new pair of Payless shoes and second-hand outfit, I walked into the office full of enthusiasm, sniffing out all the opportunities available to me. I was ready to make it on my own.

Unfortunately, I knew nothing. My managers and trainer literally had to teach me what a vacation ownership was, let alone how to sell one. There was a rotation of sales representatives, from #1 at the top to #35 at the bottom. And since I was new, I was placed at the very bottom of the rotation: #35.

In other words, I would be the last one to get an opportunity to give a "tour."[1] I had to come in to work at 7:30 a.m. and often had to wait until 1:00 p.m. to have my first sales opportunity. Most days, I did not have any opportunity to make a sale, because there were not enough tours booked. There were simply too few prospective clients for all the salespeople present.

---

1 Regarding a vacation ownership, a tour means giving a sales presentation to guests.

This set-up appeared to be a shaky start, but let me assure you that this lengthy wait was actually a gift in disguise. I was not upset that I had to wait over five hours for my chance at a tour. Rather, I was grateful to have been hired at all. I used the downtime to study, read, listen to the top sellers, and observe others' sales presentations. I was back in the kindergarten library, teaching myself.

## BECOMING PART OF THE SALES ELITE

I was determined to get to the top of the rotation.

By the second month, I was blessed that Richard, one of the top Senior Sales Representatives, took me under his wing. He observed me studiously waiting for hours on-end for opportunities to sell, and he respected the fact that I was always reading books and studying sales materials. He offered to mentor me and help me hone my selling skills.

Sometimes, we were the last ones leaving the office because we trained until 8:00 p.m. At noon, he would give me a $10 bill to buy a sandwich for us to share: tuna on wheat with extra mayo. I personally didn't care for the sandwich, but at that time, when a free meal was offered to me, it tasted like the finest lobster roll.

After a day filled with observing, training, and studying, I would go home and practice my sales presentation over and over. I practiced my body language, facial expressions, and tonality in front of the mirror. I even made my two-year-old daughter sit and listen to my presentation. As you can imagine, she was a particularly hard sell. She had the attention span of a squirrel, and she couldn't even sit long enough to hear my entire presentation before she started wandering off to look for something far more interesting. As it turned out, she was great practice for certain kinds of clients.

Within 60 days, my diligence paid off. I went from being #35 to being #1. I was the top seller in the sales department. As time went by, I started making $7,000 every month, then $10,000, then $20,000. And in my very best months, I made $75,000! In five years, I sold over $10 million worth of vacation ownerships and earned over $1 million. I was consistently the top producer for the next five years, and I was promoted five times.

When I started, I had nothing and was close to bankruptcy. But I was now able to do anything I wanted: feed my daughter nutritious foods, place her in a great school, and buy a house and my dream car. I paid off all my credit card debt (a figure that amounted to $40,000), and I was able to donate thousands of dollars to local schools and homeless shelters.

*I had transformed my life, created a bright future for my daughter, and contributed to my community—all because I had mastered a sales method. I had become a member of the Sales Elite.*

My story is unique, but I am sure that most people can recognize similar challenges that they've faced in their lives. However different our journeys may be, we have all experienced circumstances that have contributed to our character and aspirations. Those challenges become the roots of our resilience, and they can create a yearning for fulfillment. Are you ready to leverage them into your own success story?

Just like you, all salespeople have honed their own sets of skills and proficiencies, but are they truly up-to-date with all the current changes in our society? The sales industry has drastically changed over the past decade. Today, the purchases of homes, vacations, insurance policies, and other major purchases can be made online. The face-to-face sales experience is rapidly diminishing. With fewer opportunities to get in front of your Potential Clients (PCs) and sell them your service or product, how can you sustain your sales career?

Without carefully observing the changes in your sales industry and being proactive about adhering to the demands of our evolving commerce, we would be left behind, wondering where all the PCs went. This book is intended to assist you to get ahead, avoid burnout, and ultimately experience a thriving sales career. In other words, my goal is to show you how to have a more balanced life, a sustainable sales career, and more freedom to do as you please.

I congratulate you for wanting to embark on your sales journey and be a self-educator. You've probably accomplished more than you give yourself credit for. You deserve to live the life that you envision. By purchasing this book, you have already taken the most valuable first step, and you are now on the path to becoming a member of the Sales Elite.

I honor you for taking the time, funds, and energy to choose this book from thousands of options. I am excited to share my findings and my proven communication practices with you. You are about to blend your drive and talent with a sales method that will supercharge your sales career. Get ready to unleash your potential.

## BEHIND *THE 60-SECOND SALE*

In today's overstimulating world, there doesn't seem to be enough hours in the day to accomplish everything we want to do, which can quickly create a time deficit that becomes exhausting. Even as I write this, I have a basket of clean clothes that needs to be folded, sitting on my bed right now. There's always something that needs to get done: how many unread emails do you have in your inbox, how many errands do you need to run, how many calls do you need to return? I know that your to-do list can fill pages and pages. Three new items get added for every item that you cross off, don't you agree?

You already know how valuable your time is, so you can just imagine the grimaces on your PCs' faces when they hear that you want to meet with them to discuss an opportunity to purchase your product or service. It's not that they're 100% disinterested; it's likely that they've instantly weighed the benefits of listening to your presentation against the benefits of finishing their to-do list or catching up on a much-needed break to relax with family and friends.

For any successful salesperson, it is imperative to have an understanding that time and energy are becoming the most valuable commodities in today's society. A rookie mistake is assuming that all clients just want the cheapest price.

You need to realize that your clients might be willing to pay more for an item if the benefits mean that they would save time and energy. Once you have mastered a sales method that can save your clients these precious commodities, you will immediately see the difference—when it comes to your income, repeat business, and happy clients.

***The 60-Second Sale is a method like no other.***

It's recession-proof and disaster-proof. You need to follow this method with tenacity and with every fiber of your being. I've dubbed it the 60-Second Sale, but let me be clear about the context of the book: It isn't a quick fix or a get-rich-quick how-to, since these options only lead to short-term successes, if any.

As salespeople, we are usually our own worst enemies. Too often, we bring our personal issues to work and let them affect our focus, so we tend to experience huge rollercoasters in sales success: highs and lows. We also tend to lose track of what is working for us. The average salesperson tends to start disciplined and focused, then loses track soon after. Inconsistent discipline will lead to inconsistency in meeting sales goals.

Think about crash diets. They might work temporarily, but they eventually dissipate. At times, people gain even more weight than they originally weighed prior to doing their quick diet. As a member of the Sales Elite, you will begin to learn how to avoid short-term success and the downfalls of relapsing. Instead, you will focus on slow, long-term gains, where you will build a sustainable sales system that's like no other. As they say, "Rome wasn't built in one day."

Keep in mind that even though it only takes 60 seconds to deliver this dynamic sales method, it is only effective after you have learned it well, absorbed it, and developed a practice. You can easily spend hours—or even a life-time—reading this book, learning this method, practicing the exercises, and taking action in the real world to get the results you want.

*When I made $17,000 in 2004, I never thought that I'd earn $100,000 just a year later—and **half a million dollars** the year after that!*

What I am about to share with you is going to super-charge your selling power. So, silence your smartphone, stop mul-titasking, and get focused.

Your individual success will reflect your commitment to fol-lowing these steps to a "t," with no shortcuts or changes. The quality of your life—and those you are serving—depends on it. It is time for you to graduate from simply surviving the competitive world of sales, and begin to thrive and consistently surpass your sales goals, while living a more balanced life. To make the most of your experience reading this book, I encourage you to keep an open mind and absorb the concepts without judgment. Your mind is like a parachute: if you don't keep it open, it simply won't work.

I believe that there is an important reason why you've chosen this book. It is my honor to be guiding you through this method. Thank you for investing in yourself and in the people you serve.

Welcome to *The 60-Second Sale.*

# 1

# FAIR EXCHANGE

*"It's wise to give and receive fairly,
equitably, and simultaneously."*
~ Dr. John F. Demartini

●————————●

F OR ME, LEARNING ABOUT atoms and neutrons in my physical science class in high school was like learning another foreign language. It would be an understatement to say that I was completely lost. But amidst all the utter confusion, I did have one "ahha!" moment.

One afternoon, my teacher showed us a Newton's Cradle (a frame with a line of metal balls hanging on wires, which formed pendulums). As my teacher pulled the first of the metal balls and let it go, he quoted Isaac Newton's Third Law of Motion: "For every action, there is an equal and opposite reaction."

I was mesmerized as I watched the metal balls hit one another at the same speed, causing each one to move. Then gradually, they slowed themselves at the same rate. There was something about the Third Law of Motion that inspired me to research how it related to human behavior. My studies eventually led me to one of my greatest mentors: human behavior expert Dr. John F. Demartini.

In his book, *How To Make One Hell of a Profit and Still Get to Heaven*, Dr. Demartini explains that the universe is fundamentally characterized by exchange—there is a constant balance of energy at work, and that energy gets transferred throughout the universe. He writes that this principle is based on the Law of Conservation, a law in theoretical physics that states that energy is constant and can never be created or destroyed. Because the amount of universal energy is constant, the nature of the universe is to create balance. All things in the universe must have an equal balance of give and take. Dr. Demartini calls this balance "fair exchange," because energy is always an act of giving and receiving.

You may be wondering how fair exchange relates to sales. This principle is in the fiber of our industry. It defines the act of selling: giving and taking. We provide a service in exchange for payment. But fair exchange is more than just the exchange of payment for service. Fair exchange also connects our Potential Clients (PCs), clients, employers, and salespeople together in one larger system. It is at the core of all our dealings and communication. In this chapter, we will explore how fair exchange shows up in our day-to-day, as well as how it relates to appreciation, working hard, and setting boundaries.

While studying articles and books on fair exchanges, I discovered that there is a constant exchange between human beings. It can be as simple as exchanging greetings with your PCs, or exchanging your product/service for your PCs' money. In addition to these, there is also a deeper exchange occurring that is even more powerful: energy. When human beings interact, we bounce our energy back and forth between one another.

I am certain that you have felt an individual's positive or negative energy at some point in your life; they're undeniable. This experience could have occurred when you were first introduced to a new coworker. Within minutes you either felt a good vibe with this individual or an energy about her/him that made you want to cut the introduction short. In this interaction, you were experiencing their energy just as they were experiencing yours. You were involved in an energy exchange.

The exchange of energy must be balanced (fair) in order to create a sustainable relationship. You are a magnet to the energy that you radiate through your being. In the same way that someone's energy can turn you off or make you suspicious, your energy is absorbed by others. Therefore, when your attitude is negative, ungrateful, and ultimately a downer, you will repel PCs that are ready to purchase your product. PCs would rather make a purchase with a sales professional that has a positive attitude, makes them feel good about the product and organization, and is able to communicate that they will be appreciated as clients.

I consistently gave holiday gifts to the resort staff at WVO. They were the handy man, the front desk agents, and the maintenance team. The gift offerings were to let them know how much I appreciated their hard work and acknowledged them as my teammates. Because without these coworkers, I wouldn't have had a beautiful and well-maintained resort to sell. One afternoon, I had a couple who were deciding whether they were going to purchase a $60,000 vacation ownership from me. They wanted to return to their resort unit to check their finances and make a decision outside of the sales office. Prior to leaving my desk to head to their unit, they mentioned that the closet door in their bedroom didn't close properly.

When they left, I called the handy man. He had previously given me his personal cell phone number in case I ever needed his assistance. I mentioned the issue of the closet door in my PC's bedroom. He reassured me that he would take care of it.

An hour later, my PCs returned back to the sales office and sat down at my desk. They told me with excitement that they had decided to make the purchase. They shared with me that they had been sitting in the living room of their unit, discussing the pros and cons of making the purchase, when they heard a knock on their front door. When they opened the door, the handy man greeted them and said that he was there to fix their closet door and anything else that needed maintenance.

They were so impressed by the quick service that we provided as a team that they felt it was a sign for them to make the purchase with me. I strongly believe that the handy man appreciated that I had acknowledged his hard work with the gifts I gave him. In exchange, he became a reliable coworker who provided a better resort experience to my PCs and clients. Fair exchange will show up in a variety of ways. It may be in the next sale that you will make, the support of a teammate, the promotion you will receive, or all three and more. But at the heart of all of these is fairness and balance—you need to project positive energy and act proactively in order to receive it.

Giving gifts to coworkers is not the only form of fair exchange that you can give. In an ideal business world, appreciation would be reciprocal between all parties—thus creating fair exchange. As members of the Sales Elite, we must embody an attitude of gratitude. This concept may seem unrealistic for those just starting out in the sales industry, but it will shift your perspective and unleash your sales potential. Now that you are aware of fair exchange, you have the responsibility to give your best energy in every interaction at work. You will be amazed by the positive responses and support you'll receive.

Fair exchange works best when you have no expectation to receive back directly from the person to whom you gave. Think of it as paying it forward and trusting that you will receive sooner or later. Remember that nature itself keeps things in balance.

## PAPA'S GRATITUDE

I learned some of the most valuable skills in my life from observing one of the greatest men I know: my father. When I was only six years old, Papa, my older brother, and I entered a ballroom at The Hilton Hotel in Paris for the hotel employees' Christmas dinner. The venue was luxurious; glittering chandeliers, elegant mirrors, and gigantic holiday wreaths adorned the banquet halls.

I stood gazing around in wonder with my mouth open, staring at all the sparkling decorations. I was surrounded by gift boxes beautifully wrapped in Christmas paper. There was a lavish buffet laid out before us, with popular French savory dishes and a decadent dessert selection. Papa was normally a man of few words, but he worked the room as if he were the mayor. I noticed that he greeted all his coworkers with warmth and camaraderie, but when he introduced us to his managers, his strong, powerful demeanor softened as he demonstrated genuine gratitude towards them.

He told my brother and me that these men were of great importance, and that without them, he would have never held the prestigious position of "Petit Gateau Pâtissier." He was a pastry chef who specialized in small pastries and tarts, and he used his talents to bake desserts for the president of France. You see, my father came to Paris with very little, and he was a single father. Prior to his employment with Hilton Paris, Papa worked at a Chinese restaurant during the day and went to culinary school at night. He learned French very quickly and managed to graduate from Cordon Blue and Le Nôtre culinary school.

The men at the Hilton Paris Christmas party had become Papa's mentors, which is why he was honoring them. They equally respected Papa for his dedication and unwavering determination to become a master at his craft. It was a perfect example of the fair exchange of respect and gratitude.

Years later, Papa continued to show his gratitude and respect towards the clients at our family-owned restaurants in the United States. When I was out on the restaurant floor, he would often politely introduce me to his most loyal clients. He thanked them for coming into our restaurant. Papa wanted me to know how valuable these clients were to his business and in the same gesture he wanted his clients to see that their loyalty supported my father's family. I very soon understood the importance and meaning of gratitude, which was a lesson I took with me throughout my sales career.

The 60-Second Sales Method is not solely about enrolling the PCs quickly. It is about the resources and processes that go on behind the scenes, before any payment is exchanged for the product or service. Gratitude is a key piece to the domino effect of receiving a lead that will become your newest client.

If you are at the beginning of your sales career and are barely hanging on to your job because you feel lost or overwhelmed, I would highly encourage you to focus on the next part of this chapter. Even if you are a seasoned sales professional, but you feel bored, tired, or just burnt out from selling every day, take a breath. Actually, make that two or three breaths. You will want to clear your mind enough to absorb the next sales communication concept. Because if you can relate to either of these situations, you might be looking at an exit strategy. If you've been feeling overwhelmed or burnt out, I would encourage you to read this entire book before you jump ship. Because you *can* create a sales career that is uplifting and fulfilling when you take actions on all of the exercises and principles presented in this book, and especially when you embody The Circle of Appreciation.

## THE CIRCLE OF APPRECIATION

The principle I am about to share with you is so crucial that every sales professional must apply it, not just be aware of it. If you do not adopt this principle in your profession, you could eventually resent your employer or your potential clients (or both), and they are the people that support and benefit your career.

I touched on this principle a little earlier in the chapter. We will now take a closer look of how The Circle of Appreciation works. As I mentioned earlier, in every business relationship, we exchange more than just a product or service. We shift energy back and forth amongst each party involved. Have you ever heard that "emotion is energy in motion?"[2] This dance of interaction thrives when The Circle of Appreciation principle is applied. If you ever wonder why you didn't get the promotion, raise, closed deal, or return business you were expecting, then there's a good chance that you were not practicing this principle.

*The Circle of Appreciation Diagram*

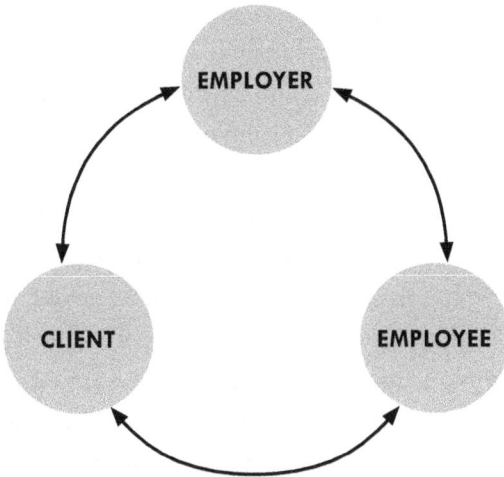

In the diagram above, the CLIENT pays for a product or service, and therefore funds the employment of the

---

2   Quote by self-help author Peter McWilliams

EMPLOYEE and part of those funds support the business of the EMPLOYER.

The EMPLOYEE provides an experience that enables the CLIENT to receive the product or service. And the EMPLOYEE enables the EMPLOYER to run its business.

The EMPLOYER receives the benefits of the EMPLOYEE's work, reliability, and productivity. The EMPLOYER provides an environment where the EMPLOYEE has opportunities to be part of an organization and earn a living, and enables the CLIENT to receive products and services that appeal to their needs and wants.

The CLIENT, EMPLOYEE, and EMPLOYER affect each other. Each one equally depends on and empowers the others.

A circle of dependence exists between all parties. Every party depends on each other's abilities to play their part and be responsible to ensure the well-being of everyone involved. Therefore, they are all engaged in a win/win/win cycle, and everyone gains. All parties involved are empowered, and best of all, everyone can benefit, achieve, and thrive. When each party involved understands, respects, and is committed to their roles and their relationship with each other, they create synergy (a whole that is greater than the sum of its parts). When you strive towards synergy in your professional dealings, sustainable earning potential is a given, and increased opportunities are bountiful.

While going to college, I was working at an upscale boutique in Fashion Island Mall in Newport Beach, CA. I was closing the cash register after a long day of folding piles of luxurious sweaters, and I overheard the assistant manager asking my coworker, "How does Aline consistently sell like a machine?"

I was ranked in the top ten producers nationwide, even though I only worked part-time. Looking back, I can see that I was unstoppable in my sales positions because I was embedded in The Circle of Appreciation practice, which was becoming my foundation for my relationships with employers and clients.

The lesson here is to appreciate your employer for the opportunities they give you, and respect them for the risks they take while running the organization. When you appreciate the PCs that have come to you, respect the opportunity to learn what is important to them, and how you can be of service, you are already well on your way to becoming part of the Sales Elite. Embodying the Circle of Appreciation means that you practice a willingness to fulfill your contribution to the cycle. You are willing to work hard, be caring in the actions you take, and dedicate yourself to consistently improving your craft. That is the essence of fair exchange. When you practice the principle of fair exchange and mutual appreciation, there will be no escaping success along the journey.

*The attitude of gratitude will enable you to consistently be a top producer.*

It is now easy for me to see that my father is the reason why I intuitively practiced The Circle of Appreciation. I truly embraced the belief that my employers had entrusted me to do my best, and in turn, their business success depended on all their employees performing at their full potential. The appreciation I had for the opportunities given to me by my past employers fueled my drive to make the most of my employment. I also considered myself blessed to have clients who relied on my top-notch service, and I was consistently a top earner because of this principle. To become a member of The Sales Elite, you must value both your clients and your employer.

## SWEAT EQUITY

Since the age of 12, I have known the meaning of hard work. By that time, my parents owned a restaurant in Westminster, CA, and I spent my weekends (and sometimes even my weeknights) there. I already thought of my stepmother as my mom, and my stepsiblings as my brother and sisters. We all contributed to the family business, which was open 7 days a week. And it still is, after 29 years of being in business.

My two elder sisters took orders, my brothers mopped and swept the floors, and my other sister and I cleaned tables and washed dishes. My mom cooked delicious Vietnamese dishes, and Papa cooked authentic French food.

At about 1:00 a.m. on a Saturday morning, my hands had gotten lost in a deep, wide commercial kitchen sink filled with soap bubbles and warm water. Suddenly, I felt a sharp pain on the tip of my left index finger, and when I pulled out my hand, it was covered in blood. I had cut my index finger with a broken cup.

My sister was waiting for me to hand over the washed cup so that she could dry it. We had work to do, and no time to waste. After patching up my finger with a Band-Aid and slipping on dishwashing gloves, my hands went straight back into the sink filled with soapy water and reached for another cup to wash.

I am grateful to have hung up my dishwashing gloves and, more importantly, to have gained the sweat equity that I experienced as a child. However, it made hard work seem like a familiar routine as an adult. My family and I are all immigrants from Vietnam, and my parents taught all of us the meaning of hard work, persistence, and dedication. Because of that lesson, we have all accomplished success in our personal and professional lives.

Sweat equity can easily be defined as simply working hard. Those that hustle and are disciplined to give their best at work every day acquire sweat equity. The more you invest in this type of equity, the more you will receive higher commissions, appreciation from your employer, respect from coworkers, and much more. These benefits occur because of the self-worth you acquire through your sweat equity. Additionally, developing your sweat equity is part of your role in the Circle of Appreciation. When gratitude and appreciation are your primary motivators, your work will improve. In exchange, the appreciation you receive from your employer will increase your confidence, which will have a positive impact on your attitude. In turn, PCs will want to buy from you, because they appreciate salespeople that are confident in their expertise as well as the organization they represent. They want to do business with those who are competent and go the extra mile. Hence, your positive energy will be a magnet for more positive energy from both your employer and your PCs. You will attract qualified PCs that are ready to say "yes" and have the finances to purchase from you.

## KOBE'S EXTRA MILE

Kobe Bryant's super-intense training regimen always put his competitors to shame. Dozens of his teammates, coaches, and admirers detailed Bryant's intense training schedule, noting that he got to the gym earlier and stayed later than anyone else.[3]

Though he was a skilled player and seemed to land baskets with ease, he regularly took hundreds of shots from all angles on the court as a warmup before each game. He was never willing to sit back and rely on his talent. He put in the hard work and was rewarded for his tireless preparation, both on and off the court. This willingness to work harder than his rivals resulted in an illustrious 20-year career and

---

3   Tony Manfred, "16 Examples of Kobe Bryant's Insane Work Ethic," *Business Insider*, 2013

earned him a reputation as one of the greatest players in the history of the game. He would not have accomplished this success without his exemplary work ethic.

As Bryant demonstrated throughout his professional basketball career, talent alone doesn't get anyone very far. Working hard, building sweat equity, appreciation for those that support your career, and appreciating your opportunities is what makes you a key player.

My parents may not be basketball legends, but I learned the value of a strong work ethic from them. When my coworkers wondered why I consistently ranked as a top producer and couldn't understand my tenacious working habits, I smiled, remembering my days as a dishwasher. I observed that if coworkers didn't appreciate our clients or the company that hired us, they would often struggle with their sales production. Seeing my father's gratitude, and how his gratitude motivated his hard work, was a crucial lesson I learned from an early age. I guess you could say that I've earned my MBA (Master's in Business Advantage) by working at my parents' restaurant.

## STAYING FOCUSED

The sales industry can be stressful, especially if your income is 100% commission-based. Despite this stress, I have often found that the top producers were also usually the most open-minded, progressive thinkers. Not only did they work hard and develop sweat equity, they also maintained a positive attitude.

This is another benefit of embodying the principle of fair exchange: when you realize that nature will make sure energy is balanced, you learn to see challenges as part of that balance. As a result, you can shift your approach to these challenges, learn to be grateful for them, and stay focused on what really matters—maintaining your appreciation and working hard for your employer and clients.

*The attitude of gratitude can help you stay focused, even in the stressful world of sales.*

## THE RABBIT AND THE HUNTER

In 2007, I was breaking sales records as a sales representative at WVO in Honolulu. This success was a shock to both my coworkers and managers because, just a few months prior, I had recently been promoted to a new sales department (In-House) and was struggling to maintain my new promotion.

However, I studied the In-House sales process and quickly caught on. I added the 60-Second Sales Method to my new process, and my sales production took off. In one quarter, I sold $1.3 million in sales, which was more volume than most sales representative had sold in a full year.

I received bonuses, accolades, and congratulations from many of my coworkers. However, at the same time, I was told that one of my coworkers had placed "a large target on my back." This sales representative was originally ranked #1 in this department. I didn't realize that I was threatening his position and reputation. This agent complained that I received special favors, such as better-quality tours, and that the sales managers favored me. I didn't accept the seriousness of these claims because I was too focused on my PCs and sales goals. Eventually, his harassment went beyond professional boundaries: he started making personal claims about my integrity to upper management.

I had to reboot this situation. By that point, the pressure from the claims I was disputing and the additional scrutiny from upper management (who supported this well-known, #1 sales representative) became overwhelming. The situation impacted my health and eventually it disrupted my sales production. This type of attention and aggression proved to be too challenging for me at that time.

I saw him as the hunter, and myself as the fastest rabbit. He shot me down, and I finally had to stop selling. A couple of months went by, and lo and behold, his sales production began a downward spiral. He made the mistake of shooting me down, instead of letting me remain healthy competition.

Instead of getting angry at him and the management that enabled him to harass me, I was grateful that he made it clear about where he stood. The most dangerous viruses are the ones that you don't know you have. Every day, I would walk into the office, glance at his desk, and quietly thank him in my head. In a way, I felt honored that I was such a threat to his sales ranking. After I focused on the gifts that this experience offered, my sales production went back up. The biggest gift was my realization that I was the main factor that controlled my sales production.

The lesson here is to accept and appreciate your adversaries in your work environment as part of the fair exchange of energy. Competition only makes you stronger, more adaptable to challenges, and more of a team player. Never shoot the fast rabbits on your sales floor. Instead, embrace them as moving targets. They will keep you grounded and hustling!

This principle alone isn't an easy fix. Practicing the Circle of Appreciation at work can be challenging, as it is unrealistic to expect all your coworkers and supervisors to believe in the same principles of mutual appreciation. You will have the usual naysayers and downers in your office. You will find negative groups of people in every organization. In addition, in a competitive work environment where sales representatives are vying for clients and positions, it can be more challenging to maintain the win/win/win dynamic as you strive to succeed. Instead of feeling discouraged, stay focused and committed upholding your part in The Circle of Appreciation. The rewards and benefits will outweigh the challenges. Later in the chapter, I will offer you several simple activities to help you cultivate this principle in your work environment.

## THE DOOM ROOM

My first day at WVO was October 5, 2005. It was another beautiful day in the paradise known as Hawaii. I walked up the steps to our showroom. I felt a mixture of excitement and nervousness, as if it were my first day of high school. I opened the door to the sales floor and was welcomed by a panoramic view of the beautiful turquoise ocean and Waikiki's pristine beach. For a moment, I had to pause just to catch my breath and pinch myself. I was taking an important step in my sales career.

My manager greeted me and took me on a tour of the sales floor, and I looked around with interest. He saved one room till the end. Before he even opened the door, he pulled me aside to a quiet space. With an expression so grave that it worried me, he said, "Aline, this is a room that you must avoid at all costs." I gulped and nervously stared at him as he continued: "Whenever you have any downtime, I strongly urge you to spend that time at your desk, instead of going into this room."

I was puzzled (if not a little afraid) as we made our way into this potentially dangerous room. Upon entering it, I heard lots of voices chattering, a microwave beeping, a fridge door slamming, and chip bags rustling. We had just walked into "the doom room": the breakroom. As my manager quickly walked me through the lunchroom, his shoulders tensed, and he held his breath as if he was afraid that we were going to catch a virus.

He hurried me out and said, "You will always find at least one person complaining about how she/he didn't get a sale. That single person can easily drag you down with them, because misery loves company." This lesson has had a very important impact on my sales success. I stayed away from the breakroom as much as possible. Instead, I quietly focused on my daily goals and self-improvement education at my desk.

Luckily, I didn't mind being perceived as antisocial. I was the newbie in the office, so no one took much interest in me. Once I became a top producer, agents begin to respect my space and routine. When you work on 100% commission, you must set boundaries, whether you are starting out in sales or a seasoned salesperson.

It can be challenging to stay focused on a busy, active sales floor. There are more than enough salespeople that would love to chat with you about unproductive topics or, even worse, all the reasons why their sales performance is off-track. Make a commitment to yourself, your employer, and your PCs: when you're at work, nothing demands more attention than your PCs and your sweat equity. You will be demonstrating the principles of The Circle of Appreciation by giving back to your employer through being responsible and reliable.

At times, it can be lonely when you're keeping to yourself in the office, but the benefits outweigh the temporary alienation. One of my mentors put it this way: "Aline, think of a marathon race. If you had an aerial view of the runners, you'd see the first-place runner all by herself. Then a few steps behind, there would be a small group of runners. And behind them, there would be a larger group of runners. But remember: *the #1 marathon winner is always alone, and only focuses on the road ahead.*"

It will be a great temptation for you to sit and vent your frustrations with your coworkers, and it is a challenge to resist these venting sessions. After all, it is so much easier to verbally harass your coworkers about why your last PC didn't purchase from you, and how it was all their fault. But you must shift your attention on more productive activities and conversations. This focus on the past and on negativity is draining, and it can spiral out of control and drag your energy down with it, like a monstrous vortex. Instead, keep your focus on your sales goals, and go in the direction that supports your success. Maintain an attitude of gratitude.

How do you make this commitment to keep to yourself, and only socialize with like-minded, supportive coworkers and supervisors? Simply ask yourself these questions:

- Will whining and complaining keep a roof over your head, put food on the table, and pay your bills?
- Will your negative coworkers buy from you when your PCs don't?

When you realize the answer is "no," ask yourself:

- Who *is* willing to pay? Who will put income in your pocket so you can live the life you envision?
- Who supports you and wants to see you win?

Invest your time and energy on your potential clients, and you will find yourself energized, inspired, and unstoppable.

Feel grateful for every opportunity, and show your enthusiasm to your PCs and your employer. Your employer gives you the chance to earn an income, provides a comprehensive benefit package, and provides a safe, clean working environment. Your PCs make the effort to show up for your sales presentation and appointments. You owe it to them to perform your utmost every workday as part of your fair exchange.

## BOUNDARIES

As you learn to enact the Circle of Appreciation in your work, you will soon understand that you need to protect your time. Everyone has their own agenda. If you don't schedule time for your high-priority goals, and the actions that are linked to your priorities every day, you will find someone else's agenda creeping into your own. Set boundaries to assist you in setting the ground rules for your fair exchanges. This way, you will avoid giving too much of yourself and depleting your energy and time. An easy technique that will assist you is to act as if you have the Hulk as your bouncer that will block any uninvited distractions from creeping into your schedule. Show up to work with purpose and direction, and reserve your energy and time for you and your PCs.

Billionaire Sir Richard Charles Nicholas Branson was once offered $250,000 to speak for one hour at a corporate event by a Fortune 500 company. Much to the surprise of the event host, Mr. Branson's office turned the offer down without hesitating.[4] But the host was persistent and called back to offer $500,000, and he reassured Mr. Branson's office that the time would be limited to just one hour. The personnel at Mr. Branson's office turned the offer down again. The host called back a third time and made a last attempt by offering more money. The personnel responded by stating that Mr. Branson had three priorities in his career, and public speaking was not one of them. Therefore, it was now clear that no amount of money could make him take the offer.

Now, you may think that Sir Richard Branson is in a unique financial position, which allows him to pass on this large earning opportunity; therefore, the rest of us could not afford to think this way. While this may be partially true, it is important to reflect on this question: How do you think Mr. Branson achieved everything he did? Like most of us, he started with very little, but because he is willing to say "no" to most distractions, he was able to focus on his priorities, propel his companies, and achieve massive success.

4   Darren Hardy, "Success Is Not About What You Do," *DarrenHardy. com*, 2010

As this story demonstrates, productivity is not always about doing more. Sometimes, it is about doing less and effectively planning your time. Early on, I realized that I had to say "no" to irrelevant opportunities and to PCs that didn't qualify to purchase my product. Then I had more time and energy for the PCs that did qualify.

Today, I continue to practice saying "no" even to the most tempting opportunities. At times, this creates friction with the ones that feel rejected by my decision. However, it benefits everyone in the end, because I am doing a disservice to someone if I say "yes" when I am not whole-heartedly committed. I would let them down either way. So instead, it is in fair exchange to be genuine and in consensus with my intentions at the very beginning with them.

Dr. Demartini stated this sentiment very clearly: "If you don't fill your day with high priorities, it will automatically become filled with low priorities." To be productive, you must be proactive.

In order to be proactive, manage your time, and live the principle of fair exchange, you need to set boundaries around your priorities. Plan out your week ahead and schedule your spare time, too. Prepare a daily plan that has boundaries in place. This technique of managing your daily activities will ensure that you are devoting time to what really matters to you. An example is below:

## DAILY PLAN

**5:45-6 am**
Wake up. Before getting out of bed, meditate on how great your day is going to be.

**6-7 am**
Get dressed and eat a healthy breakfast.

**7-7:45 am**
Commute to work, or drop off children at school.

**7:45-8 am**
Write in your Gratitude Journal.

**8-8:15 am**
Meet with your team (if required).

**8:15-11:45 am**
Make sales presentations, lead generation calls or meetings, and take 15-minute breaks periodically.

**11:45 am-12:30 pm**
Lunch (absolutely no working!).

**12:30-4 pm**
Make more sales presentations, study, and organize your work environment. Take 15-minute breaks periodically.

**4-4:15 pm**
Craft notes and actions steps for the next day.

**4:15-9:30pm**
Exercise, run errands, spend quality time with your loved ones, have some "me time," and eat a healthy dinner.

**9:30-10pm**
Settle down, and get ready for bed. Avoid using electronics because they will affect your sleep.

**10pm**
Sleep.

Adjust the activities and times to fit your life and profession. Each allotted time frame needs to have activities that are congruent to achieving your sales goals and to maintaining a balanced life. When you set these boundaries in your daily plan, make sure that nothing interferes with your activity. Obviously, if you have an unforeseen emergency, then attend to it accordingly. A disgruntled client calling at 7:00 a.m. does not constitute an emergency. The point of the Daily Plan is to ensure your time is spent proactively, not just productively.

Planning your time this way not only ensures that you keep focused, it additionally supports you to achieve massive success without burning out. This type of time management empowers you to be your best self, which benefits the Circle of Appreciation.

The boundaries that you set become the blueprint for the 60-Second Sales Method. Think of it this way: with this method, 80% of any sale is accomplished before the presentation ever begins. In the Olympics, a 100-meter dash takes less than 15 seconds, but an Olympian sprinter practices and trains for years before competing.

In a multitasking society, this Daily Plan may seem unattainable or unrealistic, and that's exactly why setting this type of schedule is crucial to staying focused and avoiding burnout. When we manage our priorities, and stay committed to them, distractions dissipate. You will soon find opportunities that will enhance your priorities. Strangely enough, people who were detrimental to your success will find someone else to bog down, and you will be left with people who respect your boundaries and want to see you win.

## AN ATTITUDE OF GRATITUDE

I started this chapter with a discussion of gratitude and fair exchange because it is the source of positive energy that matters most. When you build gratitude into your work, not only will your work improve, you will become a magnet for opportunities to earn more loyal clients. However, cultivating gratitude does not come automatically for most of us. Therefore, you need to practice gratitude daily. Like a muscle, gratitude will get stronger the more you practice. And the more gratitude you practice, the more positive your energy exchanges will be.

**DAILY GRATITUDE EXERCISE**

To develop an attitude of gratitude, practice the action steps in the exercise below. Do this exercise every morning before meeting with your first PCs. Believe me, it's worth it.

You will feel so inspired and energized that you will naturally be a magnet for success.

Here are the steps for the Daily Gratitude Exercise:

1. Get a journal and a pen.
2. On a clean page, write the date at the top.
3. Write "Dear Universe" or "Dear Life." You can also address any spiritual beings that you believe in, such as writing "Dear God."
4. Write "I am grateful for..."
5. Complete the sentence by stating a person, thing, experience, or event that you are truly grateful for. If you find it difficult to think of anything, try "the gift of life," "my eyesight," "the two dollars in my pocket," or "the clean air that I am breathing."
6. Keep writing more sentences of all the people, things, experiences, and events that come to mind until you feel grateful, loved, loving, and fully present. If you find this step daunting, initially aim for three things, then work your way up to more each day.
7. Skip a line, then write: "I am grateful now that..." Complete the sentence with your intentions for the things, experiences, and events that you want to experience in the future.

○ You need to write these intentions as if they have already occurred. For example, write: "I am grateful now that I have unexpected income of $5000 in my bank account." Or: "I am grateful now that I have booked my vacation to Greece." When you state what you will be grateful for in the future as if it's already occurred, it will reinforce your confidence and certainty.

○ Write a date next to each of these intentions—the date by which you want to achieve the event, experience, or goal. Assigning a date to your event, experience, or goal will assist you to focus your intentions into specific, trackable goals.

8. It is key that you take time to visualize and really connect to what you are writing. Avoid the use of "empty wishes."[5] Rather, be very specific and detailed. Really feel, hear, see, and appreciate what it is like to have the experiences that you want, and concentrate on those feelings of gratitude.

○ Use colorful, clear images, similar feelings/experiences/events, and even scents to make your visualizations feel more real to you. Use all your senses, really bask in the experience.

---

5   These are wishes that are not specific and believable. For instance: "I want to be an astronaut." As opposed to: "I am grateful now that I have completed three aerospace courses."

An example of one of my Daily Gratitude Exercises is below:

*Dear Universe,*

*I am grateful for the safety, well-being, and love of my family, especially my daughter and my husband.*
*I am grateful for my clean, comfortable home in San Diego.*
*I am grateful for the clean air that my family, loved ones, and I breathe.*
*I am grateful that our dog, Kaya, makes us laugh and is healthy.*

*March 14, 2016—I am grateful now that my husband enjoys paddling in San Diego. Note: Two months after I wrote this gratitude statement, my husband found a paddling crew in San Diego. He has been paddling with them for over a year now. He likes his teammates, his coach, and paddling in San Diego. During his paddling season, he ranked #1 in his crew.*

*April 6, 2017—I am grateful now that my daughter, Helena, is a contemporary and jazz dancer at a studio she loves. Note: It's been four months since I wrote this gratitude statement. As of last week, my daughter found a dance studio that she absolutely enjoys and loves.*

*I am grateful now that The 60-Second Sale book empowers 250 readers to improve their sales production and quality of life with sustainability (by 12/1/2018).*

## THE MORE YOU GIVE, THE MORE YOU GET

In every positive transaction between people, there's a fair exchange of intention, energy, and rewards. You have the power to enrich peoples' lives, including your own. During your morning commute, give someone a genuine smile, and wish them well in your heart.

Do random acts of kindness. Pay for a coffee or parking spot for the person behind you. If your financial funds are very tight, then simply give someone a genuine compliment. Get creative, and have fun with paying it forward.

The exchange that you will receive from giving will be a feeling of connection towards your fellow human beings. Continue this connection by building meaningful relationships with your PCs that are based on trust and gratitude, and you will create an epic sales career.

Remember that the attitude of gratitude is the energy that supports a sustainable relationship between your employer and clients. By being proactive with implementing fair exchanges, you will manifest the intentions written in your Gratitude List with more ease and speed, because you must give in order to receive. Your bouncer, the Hulk is ready to protect your boundaries, and you have cultivated the gratitude and appreciation necessary to work hard and stay focused. Before moving on to the next chapter, I would advise you to write down your boundaries now. Distractions will then be avoided as they tend to be the culprit for burning out. Once you've accomplished setting your boundaries you will have built your foundation to sustain your sales growth and professional development.

# 2

# DISCOVERING VALUES

*"Communication leads to community,*
*that is, to understanding, intimacy*
*and mutual valuing."*
~ Rollo May

●——————————————●

M Y BEAUTIFUL, BOLD FRIEND Jessica understood the value of investing for her retirement. At the age of 27, she began planning her investments with a well-known finance company, but her financial planner could not seem to put together a suitable plan for her.

Jessica's financial planner kept insisting that she should invest in college funds for her future children. Jessica endured three redundant meetings about this subject, and in each meeting, the financial planner kept ignoring her assertion that she never intended to have children. After much frustration, Jessica finally gave up and took her investment to another firm.

Jessica was a ready and willing client. She was standing there with her wallet open, but she walked out because she wasn't being heard. The problem? The original financial planner did not care enough to learn Jessica's values and how those values affected the way she wanted to invest her money. She imposed her own agenda on Jessia, which ultimately cost the her a qualified client, as well as all Jessica's possible referrals.

Rookies and burned-out salespeople commonly make this mistake: They treat clients as if they are a goal to achieve. They see clients as an obstacle to overcome, such as the term "closing the client." This mistake keeps the sales professional from seeing their PCs as people who have their own sets of values and vision. This type of separation creates a hole where connections are lost and, even worse, where trust is broken or never created. Instead of choosing a philosophy of "closing clients," choose to build a bridge that embraces your PCs' individualities and honors their values.

When salespeople impose an agenda (their company's, their supervisor's, or their own) on PCs, they are losing opportunities to build a dynamic and sustainable sales career. The people that must be served, first and foremost, are the PCs. Without new clients, a business cannot flourish and maintain a market share, which will have a devastating impact on the salespeople of that organization. Salespeople are responsible for respecting their PC's values at all times and making it a priority to serve them first.

*Consumers buy from you based on THEIR perceived need or want of your product/service.*

## COMMON MISTAKES

Here are the three most common mistakes that many rookie and desperate salespeople make:

1. They don't listen to the individual needs and wants of their PCs.
2. They tell the PCs that they're "wrong." Most salespeople want to prove that they're "right." OK sure, you'll be right, but you'll also be broke!
3. They tell the clients that "that's the way it should be," or, "I am more experienced than you." They want to be the expert, but in reality, they are demonstrating a costly lack of empathy.

Certain salespeople make these mistakes because they are either rushing through their sale presentations, have commission breath which stinks of desperation for a new client, and/or have their egos in their way. These behaviors will ultimately result in lack of commissions, quitting the position, or even getting terminated.

Values are like fingerprints: we all have them, yet they are unique to an individual. No set of values is the same as anyone else's. What all values have in common is that they help shape our expectations of ourselves, others, and the world around us. Being aware of this principle is going to have an impact on the way you facilitate your sales presentations.

A salesperson that attempts to bypass discovering, understanding, and respecting their PCs' values will struggle. They will be wasting their time, efforts, and energy on a dead end. As a member of the Sales Elite, you will take the initiative and time to understand your PC's Highest Values and then connect them to your product or service. Investing the time in discovering your PCs' Highest Values will assist you in learning how to enroll new clients more quickly.

## HIGHEST VALUES

We prioritize our values in sequence: from most to least important. For the sake of keeping this concept simple, I will focus on our top three values (our "Highest Values"). They may be intangible qualities (such as liberty), tangible objects (such as cash), or specific people (such as family members). These values are the things that drive us.

It is natural for us to live in accordance with our Highest Values, and we display this trait through the way we act, react, perceive the world, and are inspired.

For example, my #1 highest value is my immediate family: my husband and daughter. You might assume that absolutely everyone with a family has this as their highest value, and your highest value might also be your spouse and children. However, while that might make us similar, it does not make us the same. We have different experiences and knowledge, which means that our understanding of family is different, and the values of our individual family members differ as well. We need to peel back the layers, direct our attention to each other's values, and attempt to respect and understand them.

Let us take a closer look at my family's values:

- My daughter loves to dance, especially ballet, contemporary, and jazz.
- My husband loves to be in the ocean, either surfing or paddling.

Let's say that in your life:

- Your child's Highest Values might be soccer and video games.
- Your spouse's Highest Values might be fishing or watching football.

You and I have different values because your family's Highest Values are likely to be different from mine, and those differences impact our lives in both subtle and dramatic ways.

I have found the fastest way to discover the Highest Values of my PCs: by asking specific questions and observing the common threads in their behavior.

To understand how to naturally ask these questions, let's first take a look at your values. Note that even though you might think that you know them already, your values change over time. Your list my surprise you, and most importantly, it might give you clarity about who you are and what you stand for.

## CLARITY IS POWERFUL

It is important that you do an inventory of your own values, because these values become the basis of your "Why?" Your "why" is the reason you are driven to do and be more every day. Knowing your why will not only keep you focused in achieving your goals, it will also reveal the values that you have that may be similar or different to your PCs. When you know your values, you can connect more easily to PCs that share those values and also recognize when those values are getting in the way of building a connection.

Take an inventory of your own values by answering these questions below, and be as specific as you can:

1. What kinds of things fill your space at home, at work, apps on your smart phone, and in your car? If you have a library of books, magazines, or DVDs, what subjects are they? Do you have lots of pictures on your walls or desk? If so, what are they pictures of?

2. What do you spend your money on? (Look back over your bank account and credit card statements for the past year and review your spending.) Are you spending money on traveling, eating out, fashion, cars, or electronics?

3. Refer back to your answers for question #2. Break down those answers by asking yourself who you are spending your money on or with.

4. What subjects do you frequently discuss with friends, family, or coworkers? For instance, do you enjoy talking about certain people, professions, wealth, politics, recipes, or traveling?

5. What subjects interest you enough to ask questions and do research?

6. What kind of media are you drawn to? If you watch television or Youtube videos, what are they about? If you read and post on various social media feeds, what are they about?

7. How do you use your energy? For instance, do you enjoy fitness, traveling, hanging out with friends, working, or shopping?

8. When you're busy, what do you consistently find time for?

9. Who do you choose to spend your time with?

10. What or who is constantly on your mind?

Now that you have answered these key questions, look for patterns in your answers. Is there any repetition of words, or are there themes emerging? What are the common names, objects, or activities? Circle the most common words and names, then list them separately. For example, if the word "travel" comes up the most, add the total number of times it comes up. Once they have been added see the top three highest numbers and place a star next to them. Voila, these are your Highest Values.

You will notice that your Highest Values consistently show up when you take an inventory of the activities that you participate in, the constant topics of your conversations, and the areas in which you exert the most energy, assets, and time.

When I did this exercise, my daughter's and husband's names came up often, and so did "learning about business/finances" and "empowerment."

As it turns out, my Highest Values are:

1. My daughter and husband
2. Financial wealth
3. Transformation through empowerment

If you notice that your Highest Values are not showing up in all areas of your life, you can take the initiative to work them in. Then, you can change from feeling forced into situations (such as having to do activities that bore you or stress you out) by turning them into activities that inspire you. Begin to be aware of how your Highest Values are connected to those mundane activities. When you're experiencing challenges in any activity, link your Highest Values to the experience. I often have my daughter see how math and science are linked to her pirouettes and other dance moves.

The key to quickly converting your PCs is to determine their Highest Values (HVs). Once you have discovered their HVs you will then observe where you can link their HVs to your product/service. The link is what I call "Dominant Buying Values" or "DBVs." For example, my Highest Value is my daughter. My DBV would be linking the benefits and features of your product or service to my daughter's dance and cheer activities. When you link their DBVs to your product or service, you will personalize the benefit that your PCs can have by speaking to their HVs. Additionally, you will be able to bypass most objections and increase your opportunity to enroll your newest client.

If I were buying a car, I would need to have my DBVs discovered and linked to a car in the sales lot to help me make the purchase. The salesperson would need to ask me questions to subtly identify my DBVs.

These questions would be:

*Why is buying a car important to you?*

*Who will be driving the car?*

*Who will be transported in the car? To where do you drive most often?*

*What do you expect from the driving performance of the car?*

*Which of these is most important to you: safety, comfort, technology, or gas mileage?*

Notice that none of the questions mention cost and affordability. The reason why we avoid asking about cost or budget is that we must first understand our PCs Highest Value (HV). PCs will invest more in what will serve and support their HV. If finance is part of their HV, then the PCs will most likely tell you that they just want a good deal. In Chapter 6, you will learn 7 Key Questions that will assist you in forming the questions you need to ask your PCs.

Back to my example of buying a car, once the salesperson has asked questions and discovered my HVs (family, financial wealth, and empowerment), she/he would then link the benefits of the car to my DBVs. She/he would mention:

1. *How the car would appeal to my husband and daughter.*
   They would promote the fact that it would be great for family trips, comfortable and roomy for transporting watersports equipment, and safe for long road trips to dance competitions.

2. *How it would support my business, be of financial benefit to my family, and contribute to building my wealth.*
   They would highlight the fact that it is reliable, durable, has a high resale rate, and is economical.

3. *How it would enable my commute to public-speaking engagements, where I empower sales professionals.*
   They would point out that it comes with road side assistance in case I am driving alone, and it is spacious in case I need to drive my team with me.

These factors would make all the difference, and would likely increase the amount of money I would be willing to spend on that car. If I felt that a sales professional understood my HVs and used the 3 points listed above, it would highly increase the chances that I would make my purchase from them, rather than their competitors.

Earlier I had you follow an exercise where you discovered or re-affirmed your Highest Values. It is important that you understand how to arrive at learning your own values so that you can apply similar questions to your PCs. In addition, knowing what is most important to you, your "why," keeps you focused and disciplined in achieving your sales goals.

One might think that discovering a PC's HVs is easy—that is it no more than common sense. If that were true, then 20% of the salesforce would not be making 80% of the sales. Instead, the ratio would be far more balanced. Truly listening is an art that very few salespeople have mastered.

## LISTENING IS VITAL

Listening is a skill that is vital for enabling you to find your PC's HVs.

That said, the art of listening is a dying one, which I don't think is necessarily our fault. We are living in the 'loudest' time period in human history. I'm talking about the white noise created by the constant connection with technology: the pings and alarms and alerts and streaming videos and 24-hour news cycle.

Listening to your clients shouldn't seem like a revolutionary idea, but in this day and age, it might as well be rocket science. We are living in a time when many people have shut off their natural ability to simply listen to each other. Often, we tend to cut people off when they're talking—which is a defense mechanism that we've developed—because we're exhausted from the constant distraction of all of that noise, or we're just overwhelmed by having to hear so many things at once.

So be the change you seek. Embrace your natural ability to listen. When everyone is running one way, run the other! In a room full of people wearing drab grey, dare to be the one wearing a fuchsia leopard print. No, don't really wear that unless it's actually your style, but do catch the attention of clients by simply being different. In a world full of constant distractions, we are in need of the most basic gift, which is also the most incredible and powerful: to be heard with someone's full attention. Your clients crave this attention.

We all listen in our own ways. Just as we communicate verbally in many different styles, everybody comprehends information in a different manner. If you can identify how you listen, you can leverage this knowledge into becoming a better listener, and therefore a more extraordinary member of the Sales Elite.

Below, I have listed 5 different types of listeners, which will help you determine your own listening behaviors and, hopefully, help you avoid some of the poor listening habits I've detailed.

## THE 5 MAIN TYPES OF LISTENERS

### PARROT LISTENER

Just like parrots, these listeners repeat the things you say as soon as they hear them. They'll make encouraging noises like, "Uh-huh. Yep. Really? No way! Keep going." They might also laugh out loud every time you say something, all in an attempt to make you feel heard. They are giving you all the signals that they are listening because you're hearing them chirping in some form. However, they're too focused on managing their impression and therefore cannot be truly listening to you.

### JUGGLER LISTENER

When you're talking to this kind of listener on the phone, you can hear them typing in the background. And when you're talking to them in person, you might notice that they're also texting, glancing at other people, or watching the latest YouTube video of cats. They might think that you have x-ray vision because you sense that they're distracted, but they will often insist that you do in fact have their full attention.

### TENNIS LISTENER

This type of listener has a rebuttal for everything they hear. Every reply starts with the word 'but,' which they use to launch into their own story. Or they turn the attention to themselves: "Oh, me too. Listen to what happened to me..."

**PROJECTION LISTENER**

Before you have a chance to explain your own point of view or finish a story, these listeners quickly assume that they know exactly what you are saying, and they project their own opinion onto you. Then they launch into correcting and advising you, instead of simply listening.

**PRESENT LISTENER**

This kind of listener is a true gift! They are fully present, absorbing everything they hear without judgment. These listeners are a rare find. You can feel that they're empathetic and caring, and you want to tell them more. This type of listening is the key to becoming part of the Sales Elite.

If you think you're anything except a Present Listener, it isn't the end of your sales career. During the course of my twenty-year career in sales, I have found that a majority of my fellow sales professionals fall into the first few categories. They think sales is all about talking, so they deprioritize listening. But the ideal way to become a member of the Sales Elite and master the 60-Second Sales Method is to exclusively be a Present Listener.

If you are unfamiliar with how to be a Present Listener, you can easily acquire this skill. It simply requires awareness, practice, and patience. In college, I took a speech class and was completely surprised that we focused on learning how to listen, instead of learning how to speak. From that point on, I have been fascinated with the subject, and I am constantly working on improving my listening skills. I started devouring books on listening, completed listening seminars, and practiced with anyone who was seeking an ear.

I knew that my efforts were paying off because I began to receive feedback that I was a very good listener. I wanted a real challenge, so I practiced listening to my friends on the phone—since you can so easily multitask without the listener being able to see you. In fact, I was being such a great "Present Listener" that they kept asking, "Aline, are you there?" The silence made them think that I must have dozed off, or that the phone line was disconnected! Once they got used to the way I listened to them, they were assured that I was fully present. Then I couldn't stop them from talking and sharing their stories and feelings.

Too often, salespeople want to save time by jumping to a conclusion about what they think their PCs want. This behavior results in their PCs leaving without making a purchase (like Jessica in the earlier example), or it adds unnecessary minutes (if not hours) to the sales presentation. By assuming their PCs' values and talking without being a Present Listener, the salesperson is taking one step forward and two steps back. The Sales Elite avoids assuming what their PCs want to purchase, and instead asks questions until they have obtained sufficient information to suggest the best purchase options for their PCs.

Starting in 1986, Oprah Winfrey interviewed over 28,000 guests on her well-known talk show. While Oprah is famous for being able to unleash the inhibitions of her guests, she provided a seemingly intimate environment, where her guests felt comfortable being open and honest. I started watching *The Oprah Winfrey Show* in the early 1990s, and I noticed that she mostly listened, rather than talked, to her guests.

*Encourage your PCs to talk 80% of the time.*

Prior to my career at Wyndham Vacaton Resorts (WVO), I was seeking an opportunity to be a sales representative with three companies: Hilton Vacation Club, The Westin Vacation Club, and WVO. I pursued employment with these highly reputable companies, and I interviewed with all three companies. All three of them told me that I needed relevant experience to be hired.

I kept on pursuing WVO, only because they didn't tell me "no" outright, which meant that there was a possibility of them saying "yes." Six months later, I finally got another interview with two managers, Darrin and Terrence, who eventually became my mentors. They interviewed me, and within the same day, I was hired. They later told me that they mainly hired me because I was a "great listener."

## ACTION STEPS

To become a Present Listener, consistently follow this simple process:

### BREATHE

- Go to a quiet space.
- Close your eyes.
- Start by listening to the loudest noise you can hear.
- Focus your attention on quieter noises until the only thing you can hear is your own breathing.
- Listen to your breath moving in and out.
- Feel your chest expanding after you take in each breath. As you release each breath, let your worries dissipate, along with your monkey brain.[6]
- Fill your lungs with air, and feel your ribs and diaphragm rise and fall. Place your hand on your belly, and feel the rhythm of it moving up and down.
- Repeat this exercise for a few minutes, at least 5 times a day. Through repetition, you will master it.

### OPEN YOUR HEART

- When you are listening to your PCs, visualize your mind and heart opening up to them.
- This step is easier when you straighten your shoulders, open your chest area, and keep your palms facing up in an open gesture. You can subtly implement this posture.

---

6   Monkey brain is a mind that is not focused. It keeps jumping from branch to branch. It's a term that is often used in many other self-help books.

- Your body language will tell the person talking that you're open to listening, and that you're interested in what they have to share with you.
- Subconsciously, you will be less resistant to hearing them, and their information will move from your head to your heart.
- If you're listening to your PCs on the phone, know that even if your body is not visible, your body language is still communicating to them.

## CLARIFY

Once you believe that your PCS have finished expressing their thoughts, count to five in your head.

- To clarify, ask them a question that relates to what they have just said, such as:
  - Why do you feel this way?
  - What makes you think that?
  - I heard you say that _____. Did I understand you correctly?
- Make sure that you show a genuine interest in getting a clearer picture of the PC's point of view—without judging them.
- Always maintain curiosity. Remember that people love talking about their HVs. Selling can be easy if you let your PCs tell you exactly how and why they want to purchase from you!
- When your PCs are talking, pay attention to names, words, and events they repeatedly say. They are revealing their HVs.

**GIVE**

- Practice honoring people by giving them time, energy, focus, and patience. Just be with them.
- Before listening to someone, set a clear objective for yourself that you will give them your full attention, moment by moment.
- Let them know that you respect them and value the time they allotted to share their opinions, thoughts, stories, and feelings with you.

Now that you have the methods to become a Present Listener, it will become easier for you to clearly communicate. In contrast to most commonly held "wisdom," it's archaic to think that that a great sales professional can "talk up a storm." Instead, let your PCs do all the talking. The majority of words coming out of your mouth need to be questions and clarifications.

It would be wise for you to practice these techniques for becoming a Present Listener. You can do this by not only using these techniques with coworkers and supervisors, but with people outside of work as well. Before you know it, you will be building it into a habit and being a Present Listener will be the only way you listen.

## BE INTERESTED, INSTEAD OF INTERESTING

A sales manager once told me a story that had a positive impact on my career. After he was invited to a dinner banquet, he started a conversation with the stranger sitting next to him. Throughout the night, the stranger kept talking about himself, and my manager kept asking clarifying questions. By the end of the banquet, the stranger stood up, pointed at my manager, and said to his friends at their table, "Hey everyone, meet my new friend!"

My manager told me that this stranger knew almost nothing about him. All he had done was let the stranger talk about himself the whole night. By being a Present Listener and asking clarifying questions, he had connected with this stranger, and the stranger now considered him his friend.

While it might be over-ambitious to assume that a PC will feel like you are a new friend, she needs to be comfortable enough to open up and be vulnerable. You want to quickly earn her trust, which is achievable by remaining present while you're listening. Once you have practiced being a Present Listener, you will begin to notice that you have connected with your PC faster than ever before. This will enable you to convert more PCs into clients, reach your sales goals, and end your workdays with more energy and free time.

To learn how to connect with someone quickly, practice being curious. You can achieve this by asking these types of statements and questions in order:

1. Welcome to (name of your company or location)!
2. Thank you for visiting us today, or, thank you for joining us today.
3. What brings you here?
4. Great! We can definitely answer your questions and assist you with (the product/service you're selling).
5. First, I always like to get to know a little bit about our guests so that I can cater my presentation/demonstration specifically to you and save you time. Is that ok?
6. Is this your first time inquiring about (the product/service you're selling)?
7. What interests you about (the product/service you're selling)?
8. Ask another layer of questions that is related to their answers. (Ask questions that will help discover the "*whys*" behind their interest of your product/service.)
9. Focus on *personalizing* your questions based on the answers they gave you. (By now you will have enough information that points to their HVs and DBVs.)

You will be able to formulate your own set of questions with ease once you've read the upcoming chapters and memorized the 7 Key Questions in Chapter 6. Being a Present Listener and building trust with a stranger in a short amount of time may seem like an unreachable goal. Let me assure you that we dive further into the "how-to's" in Chapter 7.

In the next chapter, you will meet The 4 Main Personality Types. Learning about these personality types will enable you to bypass having to ask your PCs too many questions. Once you are aware of the different personality types and how to spot them, you can ask much more specific questions and connect more quickly.

CHAPTER

# 3

# THE 4 MAIN
# PERSONALITY TYPES

*"You must be shapeless, formless, like water. When
you pour water in a cup, it becomes the cup. When you
pour water in a bottle, it becomes the bottle. When you
pour water in a teapot, it becomes the teapot. Water can
drip and it can crash. Become like water my friend."*

~ Bruce Lee

A T THIS POINT OF the book, we have discussed that
fair exchange is part of how nature keeps our world
in balance, from the laws of the universe all the way down
to our interactions with people. Then we uncovered how
each and every one of us have a set of Highest Values that
are individually unique, like our finger prints. Now you
are about to be introduced to the personality types that

your PCs will fall into. I am very excited to share with you the characteristics and traits of these personalities in this chapter. Understanding the information in this chapter has assisted me tremendously in not only my sales presentations but in my personal relationships as well.

You may have noticed that you connect more easily with one type of PC: the ones with a similar personality to yours. It's easier to enroll PCs that you understand and feel comfortable with because they remind you of yourself. However, with other PCs, who have different personality types than yours, it is more difficult for you to quickly make a connection. It is often said that we tend to like people that are similar to us. But in sales, it is detrimental to avoid connecting to other personalities.

Before you start expecting to break sales records and become a member of the Sales Elite, make sure that you learn all 4 Main Personality Types. If you only understand PCs with your own personality, how can you expect to quickly connect with the other 3? If you can't connect with 75% of your PCs, you'll lose sales before you even start your presentations. In other words, learning what makes all your PCs turn on and off will push you over the very thin line between not connecting and connecting.

In this chapter, you will learn the characteristics of the 4 Main Personality Types: The Analyst, the Controller, the Promoter, and the Supporter. You will then be able to assess a PCs' personality type in seconds and adjust your personality to match theirs. This knowledge will enable you to establish quick bonds with your PCs, which will make it easier for you to enroll them.

Remember, PCs tend to trust sales representatives that are similar to them. So, let's discover the specifics of each personality type.

## IDENTIFYING THE 4 MAIN PERSONALITY TYPES

What personality type do you have? And what are the personality types of your PCs?

In order to find out where you want to go, let's first pinpoint where you are. Start by viewing the diagram below, which contains four traits and corresponding quadrants.

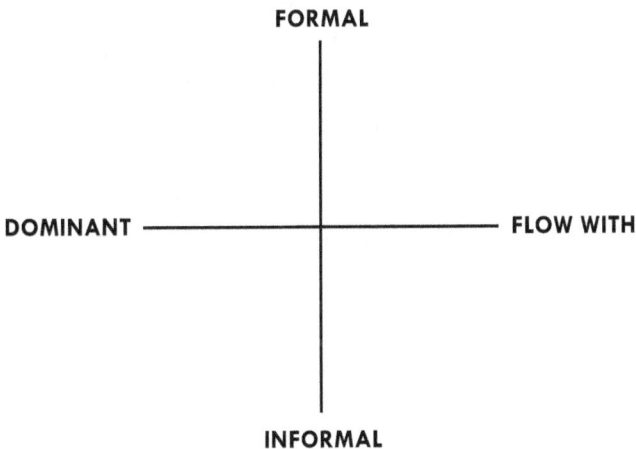

**FORMAL**

**DOMINANT** ———————————— **FLOW WITH**

**INFORMAL**

To see which personality type you are, follow these steps:

- Are you more *formal* or *informal*? Do you prefer to follow directions and rules, or would you rather figure things out as you go? Do you easily get emotional, or do you like to keep your emotions in check? If you like structure, are well-organized, and prefer to set clear expectations, you are more formal. If you dislike structure, tend to be spontaneous with people, and prefer to be highly interactive, you are more informal. **Circle either *Formal* or *Informal* in the diagram.**

- Are you *dominant*, or do you *go with the flow*? Do you take control, or do you tend to fall in line? If you tend to act assertively, want things done your way, and often take charge in a group situation, you are more dominant. If you tend to be reserved, prefer to be easy going about making plans, and often think before you speak or act, you are more flow with. **Circle either *Dominant* or *Flow With* in the diagram.**

- Place an X in the quadrant between the words that you circled. For instance, here's where my X would go:

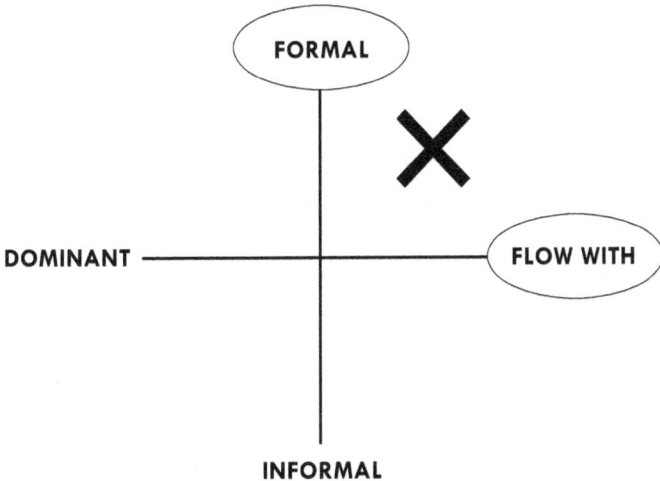

This personality classification does not mean that you have none of the traits in the other quadrants. It merely shows your most dominant traits, and the personality you are most comfortable with showing a majority of the time.

## PERSONALITY TYPE FORMULAS

You can determine your personality type according to which quadrant you placed the X in. Simply refer to these formulas:

Formal + Flow With = Analyst (task-oriented)
Formal + Dominant = Controller (task-oriented)
Informal + Dominant = Promoter (relationship-oriented)
Informal + Flow With = Supporter (relationship-oriented)

Task-oriented personality types (Analysts and Controllers) tend to be doers and reflect internally. They spend most of their energy and focus on taking care of tasks than on building new relationships. Spending quiet time to themselves is important to them so that they can check more items off their to-do list(s). At times, they may even express their care for their relationships by doing tasks or activities for people, such as running errands for someone, organizing a party or a vacation, or simply taking over a project.

Relationship-oriented personality types (Promoters and Supporters) tend to be emotionally expressive. They like to spend their energy and time on building their relationships and creating new ones. You will rarely see them alone at gatherings because they like to be surrounded by people. The Promoter tend to be the epicenters of conversations and the Supporters will be listening intently to them.

Let's meet the 4 Main Personality Types and learn more about their likes and dislikes. The following guide will enable you to distinguish your PCs' characteristics so that you can avoid repelling them and instead begin to quickly connect.

# PERSONALITY MAP

### THE ANALYST

The Analyst is often a challenging personality type to enroll. They take their time and want to analyze every available piece of data before making their decision. You can rely on the Analyst to give you an informed decision based on their endless research.

Being an Analyst myself, my favorite word is "research." If my husband asks me out to dinner, I reply: "I'll research restaurants in our area". Yelp is my go-to resource because I can read reviews, browse through photos, and read restaurant tips.

Guess who plans our vacations down to the finest detail? Yours truly has most recently planned a European trip, taking in 3 countries and 7 cities in 17 days, all without a hitch.

### *Character Traits of Analysts:*
- Want to research before making decisions.
- Never seem to have enough data, statistics, and calculations.
- Need proof of trust before they want to buy.
- Want to compare purchases with competitors.
- Move slowly and need time to process data.
- Are quiet, loyal, and reliable.
- Resist authority, and certainly avoid being wrong and making mistakes.
- Can seem arrogant because they tend to know a lot of facts, and don't hesitate to share them.

### Analysis of Analysts

To connect with an Analyst, you must first understand why they have those traits: Their purpose is to protect themselves and their loved ones.

They are fearful of making a mistake that will burden their family, friends, and employer—not because they want to be a pain or annoy you. Rather, they truly want to avoid future headaches and regrets. The irony is that they do end up with regret because their fear of making the wrong choices can often cause them to miss opportunities.

Analysts need to be enabled to take more risks and let go of worries. Therefore, as a member of the Sales Elite, your duty is to do the Analyst a favor: prevent them from missing out on an amazing opportunity to benefit from the product or service you're selling.

What makes you a member of the Sales Elite? Your commitment to being patient and persistent with your analytical PCs, and the fact that you always offer them options. It is a good idea to offer them three different choices, but no more. Offer them one option that is below their means, another that is exactly what they want, and a final one that is above their means.

Note: Ironically, the easiest way to enroll an Analyst is not by bombarding them with facts, figures, and data. Yes, give them a couple of comparisons and just enough facts to satisfy their craving, then lead them into the Promoter personality (see below). Help them get out of their head and into their heart. Get them to laugh and enjoy themselves with you. This technique will shift their focus, which enables them to just "be," rather than focusing on their worries.

If we look deeply into the 4 Main Personality Types, an Analyst often has a hidden (or wannabe) Promoter side. Too often, Analysts rely on data to make decisions, so they sometimes get tired due to the burden of making careful choices for the greater good. They will have more difficulty making a decision to purchase if they're overanalyzing their options. Instead, they need to bring out their Promoter side—relaxing, enjoying life, and being spontaneous.

### Common Objections
- Need to think about it.
- Need more time.
- Need more information.
- Need to do research.
- Out of their budget.
- Heard or read bad reviews.
- Will wait for the new model.

### How to Spot an Analyst
- Will make eye contact initially and may avoid eye contact if they're uncomfortable.
- Usually dressed neat and clean.
- Speaks directly with short sentences.
- Uses facts, data, numbers, specific locations, names and/or brands when communicating.

- Will ask a lot of questions if interested.
- Could come off as egotistical ("know-it-all" attitude).
- Will be organized, such as having a pen on them, apps on their smart phone to help them be even more organized, or a wallet with designated areas for receipts, credit cards, and dollar bills.

## THE CONTROLLER

This individual is usually found in a leadership position, whether it's in the military, a corporation, or even a family unit.

Controllers are forces to be reckoned with, and they are the prime movers behind many organizations. I truly appreciate Controllers, because if it weren't for them, it would be hard for any organizational, political, or social movement to become a reality. That said, they often appreciate a job well-done, so when they see you building your sweat equity, you will be on their radar for a promotion.

### *Character Traits of Controllers:*
- Are demanding and abrupt, and make quick decisions that rarely change.
- Are visionaries and see the big picture.
- Prefer to ask questions, rather than answer them.
- Have limited patience for listening because they prefer to do the talking.
- Are clear on objectives and focused on end results.
- Get energized when they are in charge and setting expectations.

- Want their decisions to be final.
- Have difficulty with delegating, because they believe that the best results occur if they accomplish tasks themselves.

### Analysis of Controllers

When trying to connect with a Controller, the worst action you can take is trying to bulldoze them right away. This action will only cause them to puff up their stance, and attempt to control the situation even more. Instead, remain confident, and allow them to take the initial lead. In case you missed it, the keyword in that sentence was "allow." In reality, you keep control of your sales presentation by giving the Controllers space to let them have a little control over the direction of your presentation.

After Controllers no longer feel threatened, and they feel like they can be themselves, then they'll relax a bit more. At this time of your sales presentation, you will have the opportunity to start connecting with them. Think about this relationship like a game of ping-pong. The ball will bounce back and forth. In this case, your PC will take the lead, and you will respond by asking the 7 Key Questions (Chapter 6), which will enable you to regain control over the situation. You want to keep playing this game throughout the entire sales presentation.

As you hit the ball back onto the PC's side, you want to guide them into revealing who is in their heart. Just like the Analyst that is craving to expose their Promoter Side, the Controllers have a hidden Supporter side (detailed later in the chapter). What is unique about Controllers is they don't realize they're truly a teddy bear in a lion's body. The most efficient way to enroll a Controller is to enable them to reveal their softer and supportive side. You can encourage this exposure by asking them questions that cause the PC to express how they help others. Focus on the relationships that matter to them the most. Doing so will help them lower their guard and enable the Controller to release their hidden Supporter personality. Once they let you in, you'll discover their HVs and you will meet a side of them they rarely reveal to strangers. Even though Controllers are task-oriented, their hidden need is to be connected more to the relationships that matter to them.

Because of their direct nature, Controllers may appear to be unfriendly and even overbearing. It could be easy to dislike them, but it's hard to ignore their boldness and courage. And underneath their tough exteriors, you'll find driven, committed people. You have to give them credit for taking the lead when no one else is even willing to take the first step. Understand that certain relationships are very important to them and that they express this through their leadership.

### Common Objections
- No.
- Not for them.
- Not the right time.
- Will find flaws in the product or service.
- Will purchase from the competitor.
- The price is too high.
- Want to speak to your supervisor.

## *How to Spot a Controller*

- Will make direct eye contact consistently.
- Speaks in short sentences with a strong tone.
- Often speaks in the first person.
- Will be dressed in a neat fashion and clothing will be pressed.
- Won't ask too many questions. They will be direct and at times blunt.
- Could cut into your conversation by talking.
- You will feel like they're in a rush or they will show their patience is running thin.
- Will tell you what they like and don't like openly and quickly.

### THE PROMOTER

We all have that enthusiastic friend who gets us excited about an event, only to show up very late—or not all. Let me introduce you to the Promoter. Even though the other Main Personality Types can get frustrated with Promoters for their unpredictable streaks, we can't help but love their energy and charm.

## *Character Traits of Promoters:*

- Often overindulge.
- Are fun and full of energy.
- Are the life of the party and often have large groups of friends.
- Love people and adventures.
- Love to be the center of attention.
- Are disorganized, messy, tardy, and easily distracted.

- Regularly break rules and are noncommittal, even though they are driven.
- Are afraid of losing their freedom.
- Are inspiring and charming.
- Are great at start-ups, but not-so-great at finishing projects.

### Analysis of Promoters

Promoters will take you to places that you never intended to visit, and they will help you experience things beyond the scope of your imagination. They can entice you to be spontaneous and courageous, which might have been holding you back from exciting new experiences.

The challenge with enrolling Promoters is that their heads are often in the clouds. They can easily be already looking forward to happy hour, even though it's only 12:00 pm or basically eyeing the next adventure. They get caught up in the next exciting event or activity, and will quickly lose interest if they deem anything boring. Often, this personality type makes a lot of money, but has a hard time holding onto it because they're spending it on new adventures or new, shiny objects.

Promoters' hidden side is an Analyst personality. The Promoters aren't aware that their balanced side is an Analyst. To enroll Promoters, you must enable their Analyst side to come forward. Give them a fact or two, and empower them to make a decision based on their own sound judgment. This causes them to be more grounded and focus on the subject. Show them how the benefits of your product or service will enable them to have more fun and experience the excitement of life with the people that matters to them.

At times Promoters forget that not everything in life is a fun journey. They need to be reminded of the negative consequences they have experienced due to their aloofness and lack of focus and commitment. You can remind them of these forgotten challenges by asking them the Influential and Directed Questions (Chapter 6) and by being a Present Listener.

Then, show them that they can sustain the joys of life and their relationships by pointing out the challenges they've experienced in the past and linking the solution to having your product or service. Recall that Promoters thrive on building new relationships and maintaining the ones they have. Have them share their most important relationships with you and guide them to enhance those bonds with your product/service.

### Common Objections
- Don't have the time right now.
- Too much going on for them.
- Have 10 similar products or services already.
- Have friends that have your product already, so they will just use theirs.
- Will buy from you next time.
- Will tell all their friends about buying it (avoids mentioning that they won't buy it themselves).

### *How to Spot a Promoter*

- Can be loud and chatty.
- Will make eye contact at first with a smile until they get distracted.
- Charming and friendly.
- They usually initiate conversations.
- Multi-tasking is their innate reflex.
- Appear to always be in a good mood.
- Will show signs of disorganization.
- Won't remember your name at first and may even forget the topic of the conversation.
- Attracts attention and thrives in high energy surroundings.

**THE SUPPORTER**

We all love the Supporter. This personality type will stay up until 2:00 in the morning to make a batch of holiday cookies for the office party. Then they'll go around the party making sure that everyone got a cookie, even though they're sleep-deprived. And alas, they give the last cookie to someone else and keep none for themselves.

### *Character Traits of Supporters:*

- Value relationships.
- Want to be of service for the greater good.
- Avoid saying "no."
- Are eager to please and fearful of rejection.
- Are time-consumers and skeptics.
- Don't like dominant personalities.
- Can be overly sensitive, even passive-aggressive.

- Are reliable and generous.
- Are often overwhelmed and overcommitted.

### Analysis of Supporters

Controllers, Analysts, and Promoters would not be able to express their interests and do their best work without Supporters. Beside every leader, you will see a group of Supporters nearby. Supporters often work in administration, or they are teachers, nurses, or social workers. Their gift is their concern for humanity and they like to genuinely help people.

To enroll a Supporter, you must link the benefit of their purchase to that deeply held value of wanting to help people, while also enabling them to support themselves. Show them that buying your product or service will not only be useful for their loved ones, it will be beneficial for them as well. Much like the old adage that we must love ourselves first before we can love others, Supporters need to be enabled to help themselves so that they can continue helping others.

The Supporter's opposite side is a Controller. One of the characteristic traits of a Supporter is passive-aggressive tendencies. The reason behind this trait is mainly due to the hidden Controller side of a Supporter attempting to put their foot down and take back control. Assist your Supporter PCs to take back control by guiding them to a point where they give themselves permission to enhance their own life.

For example, when I worked at WVO, I would guide Supporters to see that buying a vacation property meant that they could invite relatives, family members, and friends along (who might not be able to afford it otherwise), host dinners and parties, and spend more time with their loved ones/those that they cared about. I knew that they frequently overcommitted themselves, so I would point out that their purchase would also mean that they could relax, recharge, and take time for themselves and their nearest and dearest. "After all, doesn't the Supporter deserve more pampering?"

### Common Objections
- Normally won't say "no" directly.
- Have your product or service already.
- Maybe next time they'll purchase.
- Poor timing.
- Not for her/him but will refer their friends instead.
- Will ask your business card so that they can contact you at a later time to purchase.

### How to Spot a Supporter
- Prefer to avoid direct eye contact.
- Soft-spoken and gentle.
- Great listeners.
- There is a warmth about their energy.
- Very relationship-oriented.
- Understanding and accommodating.
- Thoughtful as well as caring.
- Will say "yes" or be agreeable to most questions and comments.
- Will ask for very little, if any, for themselves.

Assuming your PCs' personality type is far from an ideal technique to gain commonality and trust. Instead, take the time to understand the characteristics that you are experiencing and observing in your PCs. Then, dig deeper by asking your PCs the Key Questions (covered in Chapter 6) that will reveal other behaviors and responses that suggest their personality type and Highest Values.

## OPPOSITES ATTRACT

My husband is literally the most extreme example of a Promoter that I've ever met. Do his character traits cause friction with my Analyst personality? You bet. He calls me "The Fun Police," and I call him "The Maverick." On the bright side, there are worse names we could call each other. Our personalities balance each other out, and we appreciate our differences. I can rely on him for fun adventures, and he can rely on me to make sure we get back home safely.

True to my Analyst traits, I had always been too afraid to go back to the country I was born in. Since my whole family fled the country after the fall of Saigon, it was rife with memories of loss and destruction. After his own visit, my husband reassured me that it was now a safe, lovely country, and he encouraged me to rediscover Vietnam.

With deep fear and nerves buzzing through me, I took my daughter to Vietnam. She was seven at the time. We visited my father's old home in Dalat, and we stayed in the beautiful beach town of Nha Trang, which mirrored the landscape of Hawaii. The food was absolutely amazing, and observing the locals made me appreciate the simple joys of everyday life.

Since that first trip, I have visited Vietnam twice, and I am counting the days until we can return. I felt safe there, and I reconnected with my roots and embedded myself more in my Vietnamese culture. I now have an immense sense of respect for everyone who has emigrated from their country of origin to a new home, just as my parents did. They have learned a new language, found a new home, and started new careers, all while acclimating themselves to a new country and culture. This feat is nothing short of amazing.

Without the encouragement and risk-taking of my Promoter husband, I may never have taken this trip, and I never would have discovered this deep well of culture, gratitude, and respect for Vietnam. My husband enabled me to unleash the Promoter side of my personality.

When you provide opportunities for your PCs to express their opposite characteristics, make sure that you earn their trust first. You may be asking them to trek on unfamiliar territory and they need to know that there is support and caring along the journey. Your PCs will need to feel that you have their best interest in mind when leading them through your sales presentation.

## PRE-EMPT OBJECTIONS

Show your PCs that owning your product or being a member of your service will enable them to fulfill a purpose that's connected to their HVs, which will be different for each of the personality types. Here's the kicker: we actually contain aspects of all 4 personalities, to a greater or lesser extent.

Recall a time in your life when you have been a Promoter, a Controller, an Analyst, or a Supporter. You may be a Controller at work, but a Supporter at home. You might have been an Analyst when you were checking your bank and credit card statements, and a Promoter when you were inviting your neighbors and friends over to your house for a dinner party.

Tap into those memories and feelings when you are dealing with someone who has a different personality type than yourself. We are not "fixed" as just one type. Rather, we all have preferences and inclinations, which can fluctuate. As Bruce Lee says, "Be like water my friend".

Learning the traits of each Main Personality Type became a priority when I first became aware of them. I wanted to have a better understanding of my PCs' preferences and dislikes, so that I was better prepared to deal with their objections when they arose.

In fact, as a member of the Sales Elite, you want to be able to preempt the situation by directly addressing the PC's common objections before they even think of them. This technique shows your confidence and that you have helped PCs just like them before. It also proves that you can empathize with their resistance, and that you have worthwhile experience. Therefore, you communicate that they are in good hands with you.

We feel more at ease when we know that others have similar challenges, fears, or opinions as our own. When people feel more comfortable with you as a salesperson, they are more open to becoming your clients.

## EMBODY THE PERSONALITY TYPES

Now that you are fully aware of the 4 Main Personality Types, you will begin to enroll more PCs into clients. Keep in mind that being aware isn't enough. Memorize all the characteristic traits of each personality and practice embodying the different personality types, so that you can shift your personality to match your PC's. You will then be able to walk in their shoes which makes you more relatable.

During your sales presentations, you want to:

1. Quickly assess your PCs' personality type by utilizing the Personalities Map, using Key Questions (Chapter 6), and by being a Present Listener.
2. Match their personality type.
3. Set the pace and take the lead (Chapter 5).
4. Empower them by drawing out their opposite personality type from the one they're more comfortable displaying (see opposite chart below).

**5.** Continue adjusting and leading until you have enrolled your PCs.

---

**OPPOSITE PERSONALITY TYPES**

Controller < > Supporter
Analyst < > Promoter

---

## INCREASE YOUR COMMISSIONS

A member of the Sales Elite can determine a PC's personality type within seconds. Let's get you on your way to increasing your commissions.

Here is your list of must-do's in order to connect quickly with each personality type:

**1.** Memorize the characteristic traits and analyses of each type.
**2.** Avoid expressing the language or behaviors that would turn off your PCs based on their different personality types.
**3.** Understand and memorize the most common objections.
**4.** Prep for solutions to the common objections of each personality.
**5.** Recall specific times where you displayed the different personality types.

Which of the 4 Main Personality Types can you relate to the most? Interestingly, when we are more balanced and congruent to who we really are, we display all 4 personalities in different situations with clear intentions. Instead of being completely blind-sided by behaviors that we may not be aware we exert, we can begin to manage our own expectations as well as that of our PCs by paying careful attention to their personalities, as well as our own.

# 4

# SUPERB CUSTOMER EXPERIENCE

*"We see our customers as invited guests to a party,
and we are the hosts. It's our job every day to make every
important aspect of the customer experience a little better."*
~ Jeff Bezos

T HE MOST CONSTANT THING in life is change. If you struggle with that reality, you might still be carrying a pager and wondering why no one is paging you back. If so, donate your pager to the Tech Museum, and get ready for a tectonic break from the old way of selling that will result in a shift in your customer's experience.

Steinway Hall is a piano showroom that's down the street from Carnegie Hall in New York City. Erica Feidner made sure that the entrance offers a welcoming experience. The showroom has been remodeled according to her specifications, which includes bright, sunny lighting to evoke feelings of happiness. An art exhibit is displayed on the walls near the pianos, and it's rotated every six weeks.

In March 2011, *Inc. Magazine* called Feidner a force of nature and rated her one of "The 10 Greatest Salespeople of All Time." However, she isn't aggressive and doesn't pressure her clients into purchasing pianos that range from $2,999 to $152,000. Rather, she caringly observes how her PCs respond to the pianos with their body language, their energy, and their answers to her questions. In addition to her *Inc.* accolades, Feidner has been Steinway's top sales representative for 8 consecutive years. In fact, she's sold over $41 million in pianos.

Feidner thinks of herself as more of a consultant who provides an unparalleled experience for each of her clients, rather than a salesperson. She makes sure that every sales presentation is carefully molded to the personality of her PCs. Perhaps this attention to detail explains why she is known as the "Piano Matchmaker."

## BRAND RELIABILITY

In today's competitive market of shoppers and consumers, salespeople are challenged daily to gain new clients and to maintain their loyal clientele. A rapidly growing obstacle is that consumers have more options for the same item or service than ever before. Think about how many fitness studios, coffee shops, banks, real estate brokerages, and investment firms are popping up in your city every year. The crowded space is not only growing around you physically, it's also on the web. Online shopping and services make this challenge an abyss of competition.

The question is, how do you let your PCs know that, though they may purchase the same item or service from your competitors, you are the better salesperson from whom to purchase? You do so by providing compelling experiences that tell your PCs the following:

- I listen to you.
- I understand your needs and wants.
- I can predict your future needs and wants.
- You can trust our brand and me.
- You come first.
- My brand and I are reliable.
- We enhance your life and those that you love.
- We face challenges for you.
- We appreciate and respect you.

The Sales Elite are part of what I like to call the "Customer Experience Movement." This type of salesperson knows that the only way to stay ahead of the competition is to do things differently. They cater to their PCs' individual needs and wants while providing what consumers crave: attention, care, inspiration, empowerment, and legacy.

You may be thinking right now that your clients don't care about any of the above things. I understand that it may be a far-fetched concept if you are selling anything but self-improvement brands. However, when we enable PCs to see beyond the actual service or product we sell and connect the benefits to their Highest Values, they will listen and pay more attention because their sales experience will be catered solely to them.

Let's say that you are a solar power system salesperson. You have a PC whose first name is Julie. Her Highest Values are her child, living a healthy lifestyle, and building financial wealth. She is a Promoter personality type. Julie's ideal sales experience would be as follows:

- **Attention**: You would ask Julie Key Questions (Chapter 6) using her child's name, a healthy lifestyle, and financial wealth-building questions. You will show interest and curiosity when asking her these questions.
- **Care**: Julie will feel heard and understood because you would be a Present Listener.
- **Inspiration**: Highlight that Julie would be a leader/pioneer in her community by helping save the environment, which will enable for her and her child to continue on living a healthy lifestyle. She could inspire her community, peers, friends, and her child to care more about the environment (you can ask for referrals after she becomes your client).
- **Empowerment**: Show how Julie and her child would have the liberty of having energy independence. She will have access to the Solar Renewable Energy Credits and increase the value of her home.

- **Legacy:** She would be showing her child how to make wise financial and environmental investments. Thank her for making an impact on helping the environment.

In addition to satisfying what your PCs are craving during their sales experience, make sure to add multi-sensory experiences. You will do this by stimulating as many of these senses as you can: sight, taste, smell, hearing, and touch. Offer them snacks, beverages, and to touch and feel your product. If you're selling a service, give them a free trial run. Make sure that your sales office smells fresh and inviting. Realtors are known to add scents to enhance cleanliness and warmth at their open houses. And recall how the smell of a new car is so effective that they even make air-fresheners with "new car" scent. Our senses are powerful, they connect us to memories and positive (or negative) feelings. Make sure you are leveraging these senses to provide a memorable and enjoyable experience for your PCs.

One brand that we can rely on to be a leader in the Customer Experience Movement is Starbucks. The next time you walk into a Starbucks, notice that they have strategically staged each shop's interior design. They have the most impressive sales process, as well as a beverage and food serving system like no other coffee shop.

In 1983, Howard Schultz, CEO of Starbucks, had his "Eureka" moment while visiting Milan, Italy. He noticed that the local espresso shops were places where people gathered and socialized. Customers took their time sipping their espressos and chatted with other patrons. Schultz took this concept back to Seattle and eventually transformed the "coffee culture" in America and systemized the experience.

Music is often used to put customers in a certain mood, or it can be used to enhance experiences to brand the organization. For example, Disneyland plays certain music on their rides to create a "memorable Disney experience." When we hear a particular song, it triggers fond memories of our childhood.

Starbucks does the same with its music. When you walk into any Starbucks, your ears are entertained by upbeat jazz music that's not too loud. There's a sense of warmth and comfort, and you can relax knowing that your favorite cup of coffee or tea will be brewed to your exact specification. There are leather lounge chairs that you can sink into while sipping your beverage and getting lost in a book or blog. Wood tables and chairs are distributed to entice you to sit, relax, and drink while chatting with friends and family. Starbucks has also become a workspace for students and for those working on the fly—not to leave out the countless business meetings that rely on it as their go-to spot.

Throughout the world, Starbucks has replicated this coffee-house experience to a "t." You could call it the McDonald's effect. You can rely on the Starbucks brand, knowing that each location will make your drink exactly to your expectation every time.

Schultz accomplished his vision by transforming coffee shops into gathering places. He created a Superb Customer Experience that makes people want to keep coming back, not just for the coffee but for the experience of getting coffee in that atmosphere. The question now is: How are you going to make that shift from just selling your product or service to providing the whole package—the sales *experience*? Before we dive into the "how," let's focus on the "why."

If Feidner and Schultz didn't get you fired up to change the way you want to provide your sales service, then take heed: The principles that I'm sharing with you in this chapter will either encourage you to provide Superb Customer Experience, or wake you up to the need to transform aggressive and hard sales tactics into humanized methods of selling.

## CAVEAT VENDITOR
Remember the old days of *caveat emptor* (buyer beware)?

In the past, a client endured almost all the risk associated with their purchase, but those days are quickly fading away. You might still encounter unscrupulous salespeople, who will dupe you into purchasing a defective or useless product or service. However, these salespeople and their organizations will not survive in this new generation of highly informed, empowered consumers.

Is your sales career dependent on PCs living in the US? If so, be aware that 84% of Americans adults use the internet, so they have easy access to information and advice from people across the planet, including links to your competitors.[7]

How does the internet presence of your PCs have an impact on your sales career? Prior to the emergence of the internet, disgruntled consumers would only be able to inform their friends and family members that they should avoid purchasing from you or buying your organization's product/service. Today, the scope of feedback on your service, character, and reputation is exponentially amplified across the internet.

Today, as members of the Sales Elite, we must respect the concept of *caveat venditor*, which is the reverse of *caveat emptor*: seller beware. We are the ones who must be aware of our responsibilities for the service we provide and the organization that we represent.

If you haven't Googled yourself in the past month, go ahead and add that action to your to-do list. What is the online feedback about you and your organization? What do your public profiles suggest about you? Are you aware that one negative review on Yelp can cost you or your organization up to 30 clients, and that five-star reviews can increase your revenue by 5-9%?[8]

---

7   Andrew Perrin and Maeve Duggan, "American's Internet Access: 2000-2015," *Pew Research Center*, 2015

8   Stacey Rudolph, "The Impact of Online Reviews on Customers' Buying Decisions," *Business 2 Community*, 2015

Set the tone, and maintain the legacy of your brand by providing experiences that go beyond your customer's expectations and positively represent your organization. Grow a personal brand with a public presence that you're proud of, and that inspires PCs to want to do business with you.

In the next part of the chapter, we will cover sales tactics that are counterproductive in providing the Superb Customer Experience that is necessary to enroll your PCs into loyal clients. You may be encouraged by your supervisors or coworkers to use these sales tactics because they may not know any other options. Once you've read this chapter, you will have the tools to choose differently and be part of the Customer Experience Movement.

How do you create experiences that go above and beyond your PCs' expectations and avoid ordinary, predictable, boring sales presentations?

## TAKE A STEP BACK

Actually, make that several steps back. Now, look at what your PCs have been experiencing.

For example, if you're selling cars, then you must be aware that most PCs drive into the dealership already wary of the group of salespeople hanging outside near the entrance. I am often surprised to still see this grouping when I drive past a dealership.

It's a given that when you walk into a car dealership, you're probably nervous and hesitant; you're on high alert about "being sold." In fact, you may feel like you're a guppy stumbling into a shark den. Could this hesitation be the reason why online car-purchasing is a growing market?[9]

Costco understands the hassles and intimidation of the car-buying experience. That's why they've created a buffer between their members and dealerships. If you preselect a car through Costco's website, they will ensure that your experience will be hassle-free. Costco makes certain that their partnered dealerships will provide excellent service. For example, the Costco program prohibits participating dealerships from selling vehicles with expired manufacturer's warranties. That one simple policy can improve the customer experience because the brand communicates trustworthiness.

Are you beginning to think of the changes you can make to your sales presentation to improve your PCs experiences? Even the slightest change can help you increase your current enrollment percentage. I encourage you to take a closer look at the experiences you and your organization are providing your PCs. Keep an open mind and withhold judgement. What is and isn't appealing to your PCs?

---

9   "Death of a Car Salesman," *The Economist*, 2015

Begin the change now by following these action steps:

1. Write down what your PCs are currently experiencing from the moment they meet you until the moment they're no longer in your company. Map out their typical experience from start to finish. Make sure to be very honest and detailed.

2. Now write down what you would want for your PCs to experience between the moments described above. Be creative and picture yourself in their shoes. What does Superb Customer Experience look like to you?

3. Brainstorm how your product/service can assist PCs achieve a life that they aspire to have.

4. Make a list of changes you can make at various steps of the process. Be specific about what you will do in the future to be focused on delivering an experience your PCs will value.

Finally, make a commitment to yourself and to those you serve: From now on, you will only provide Superb Customer Experiences by being a Present Listener, appreciating your PCs, discovering their Highest Values, and linking their DBVs to your product or service.

When practicing these steps, it's going to be invaluable for you to be flexible, and you might even be stepping out of your comfort zone. Your manager or supervisor may not understand your improved sales presentation. At times, it might be easier to beg for forgiveness rather than ask for permission. Be sensible when bending the traditional order and flow.

Change can be slow, and resistance accompanies it. I understand that your management team may not be open to altering their sales process. However, you can do your part to make changes that would respect your employer's core values while providing Superb Customer Experiences that are customized to your PCs individual preferences. To deliver a Superb Customer Experience that connects to your PC, be a Present Listener, discover their HVs, and inspire them to get what they want (and more) by linking their DBVs to your product or service.

## HELP PEOPLE GET WHAT THEY WANT

I once read an article about Mark Dickinson, who was urgently making his way from Los Angeles to Denver, CO to visit his daughter. He'd just heard that his two-year-old grandson, Caden, was dying from a head injury, which he'd incurred after his mother's boyfriend threw him across the living room. He was in a coma, but was scheduled to be taken off life support at 9:00 p.m. that evening. That way, his organs could be donated to patients in need.[10]

Mark desperately wanted to be there to say goodbye to his grandson and support his grieving daughter. Mark's wife called Southwest Airlines to notify them that he was running late on the way to the gate.

As usual, LAX had long lines at check-in and security. In fact, by the time Mark arrived at the gate, it was ten minutes

---

10 Natalie Avon, "Pilot holds flight for man going to see dying grandson" CNN, Travel, 2011

past his flight's scheduled departure time. He was trying to catch his breath and expected the plane to already be gone. To Mark's amazement, the pilot was actually waiting for him at the gate. The pilot had held the plane at the Southwest gate because he'd heard about Mark's family emergency. Mark graciously thanked the pilot.

"No problem," the pilot responded. "They can't leave without me, anyway!"

This story rightfully made headlines, and it proves that customer experiences come first at thoughtful, caring companies. Because of this heartwarming story, Southwest Airlines will surely gain many new customers. They certainly have earned my loyalty.

*Your income is a byproduct of the way you help people get what they want.*

Avoid becoming discouraged if your employer doesn't empower you to provide your own unique brand of Superb Customer Experience. Even the slightest gesture of unexpected care and respect will go a long way.

When I sold a vacation ownerships in Hawaii, I was entirely aware that my PCs only came to the sales presentations for the free breakfast buffet, the two free tickets to Pearl Harbor, or the free vouchers to a lavish luau. Most of my PCs had traveled thousands of miles across the ocean, spent thousands of dollars, and waited years to be there. I would always begin my presentation by saying, "Congratulations! You made it to Hawaii. What are you celebrating?" They were usually on the trip of a lifetime.

I made a point to shorten my presentation and be laser-focused. That way, I could provide the most effective, fun, and interactive sales presentation possible. Whether my PCs purchased from me or not, my presentation was short, effective, and entertaining. In fact, it averaged 40 minutes or less. I once made a presentation and sale within 15 minutes. I valued and appreciated the time of my PCs because I understood what they really wanted: a vacation in paradise.

A few of my coworkers would drag out their sales presentations for hours. I couldn't understand why they thought that keeping the PCs in the sales presentation longer would make them more likely to make a purchase. Perhaps they thought that holding them hostage would cause them to pay for a means of escape!

But that never happened. They purchased nothing. They left feeling annoyed, bored, and exhausted, and vowed never to get themselves into that kind of situation again. These coworkers didn't practice the Circle of Appreciation. As fate would have it, these coworkers either quit or were let go because their sales production was below the minimum.

## INSPIRATION: A REAL GAME-CHANGER

Your presentation has the power to control your PCs' perceptions of what they're buying. In other words, PCs will judge their future satisfaction with the purchase of your product or service based on their experience during the sales presentation. It's something I consider to be common sense, but unfortunately, it still isn't very common in practice.

Simply put, PCs will relate negative feelings to owning and using the product or service if they:

- Are confused about the item or service being sold.
- Are frustrated with the sales representative or manager.
- Feel disrespected or misunderstood during your sales presentation.
- Are uncomfortable in the environment and culture of the sales office.

To put it another way, a negative sales experience will cause your PCs to assume that being your client will eventually lead to buyer's remorse. If your PCs experience any of the above feelings, the likelihood of them purchasing is slimmer than the odds of winning a million-dollar jackpot, and even if they do purchase, they will often soon cancel or demand a refund.

I have studied many different sales techniques and was taught countless of sales strategies. There is a common sale tactic that involves conveying either a Fear of Loss or a Hope to Gain (or both) to a PC during a sales presentation:

1. **Fear of Loss**

   Encourages the PCs to feel that they'll miss out on an opportunity. This sentiment is often used in every form of commerce: "Limited time only!" "While supplies last!" or "Sale ends soon!" (For some reason, an exclamation point adds a sense of urgency! See!!)

2. **Hope to Gain**

   Feeds your PC's hope of gaining more than they currently have. It taps into their greed, competitiveness, and desire, and it works well with the type of person who likes to "Keep Up with the Joneses."

I've tested both of these sale tactics with my PCs, and although I have occasionally found them to be effective, they are not always reliable. The two mindsets above are not a sustainable way of attaining happy clients and repeat business, and they will often lead to a client changing their mind and asking for a refund. In other words, they get buyer's remorse.

As a young adult, finally making a little extra money to invest in a gym membership, I visited my local fitness club. The sales person sat me down after a short tour of the equipment and the facility. I didn't feel comfortable at this particular gym and felt even worse when the salesperson said, "If you don't sign up you can die. You don't want your health to get so bad that you'll die, right?" His question made me feel even more out of place. I was shocked by how his presentation went from, "Take a look at our newest equipment," to, "You don't want to die, right?" He was using the "Fear of Loss" tactic, and was not at all interested in my own HVs. I got out of his cubicle and headed out the door in a flash.

If you rely too much on the sales tactics listed above, it can make the salesperson appear to be aggressive, petty, and lacking in genuine empathy. It depletes the possibility of building a loyal clientele. Instead of using these short-lived tactics, there are better ways to operate, even though you might have been trained to use the one above.

Rather than motivating your PCs through fear, encourage interpersonal connections through enabling them to share their Highest Values, tapping into their inspirations and aspirations, and creating a positive state of being. You will notice that your PCs will give you repeat business and refer you to more clients like themselves. Additionally, you will receive referrals of their friends and family members that are eager to buy from you.

Yes, it might sound super-cheesy to you, but stop and think about the last time you purchased an item or an experience because you felt like your needs were being heard by the salesperson. Think about the feeling of buying something because it made part of your daily life easier or more enjoyable. It supported your Highest Values.

If you repeatedly purchase from the same company (or better yet, the same salesperson), you know what it takes to become a loyal client. Provide the same Superb Customer Experience for your PCs that encourages their loyalty.

In short, to inspire your PCs, you must first:

- Find out how your product/service would enhance their lives. Learn about their Highest Values, their wants, and their fears.
- Empower them to give themselves permission to live the life they deserve (even if they don't believe they do). I often must let my PCs know that they deserve the benefits of my products. Then they'll give themselves permission to buy something for themselves.
- Encourage them to have the experiences and moments they didn't think they could.
- Be the person who sees them as bigger than they are. Show them that they're more powerful than their fears.

Initially, PCs that come to your sales presentation have some interest in purchasing your product or services. Their experience with you during their presentation communicates either warning signs to exit or reassurance to proceed with the purchase. In short, create a space of trust, fun, aspiration, and support so that your PCs can live in accordance to their Highest Values through using your product or service.

## ASPIRATION: ENROLLING YOUR PCS

It is not enough to sell a product/service. Offer your PCs something that not only improves their lives but let's them see the bigger picture. Are you selling a gym membership, or enrolling them into a healthier life style? If the fitness club salesperson had focused on my own aspirations for joining a gym rather than trying to scare me into an enrollment, my initial interest would have been converted into a sale. The key with being aspirational is to connect your product to the life your PC *wants to have*, which is not the same thing as saying, "buy this or else."

Once you have built rapport with your PCs and you have discovered their HVs, you can begin to uncover any disconnects between the values they communicate and the life they currently have. This is not the same thing a creating a non-existing problem, it is simply shining a light on an area where their life can be improved in accordance to their Highest Values. You can then address these disconnects that your PC may not have anticipated. The mismatch would be solved by using your product or service. The key is to empower your PCs to realize, on their own, that what you're offering would solve those problems without you pushing or pressuring them to realize it.

A coworker, Aly, once told me about a realization he had after work one day. He was feeding pigeons at the beach park. He noticed that when he threw bread crumbs directly at the pigeons, they would be scared and fly away. However, when he threw the crumbs slightly away from him, the pigeons were interested and slowly made their way closer to the crumbs, and closer to him.

The point is avoid throwing your product or service directly at your PCs. They will feel pressured or turned-off. Instead give them bit by bit of information mixed with the benefits and link those benefits to their DBVs. Then shed light on the disconnect that they were not aware existed and let them resolve it by choosing to purchase from you.

When I worked at WVO in Honolulu, I branded myself as an expert on Wyndham Vacation Resorts VIP Ownership. I studied the program inside and out, and learned as much as possible from VIP Owners who toured with me. I knew that being treated like a VIP was something that my PCs would value.

When my PCs sat down with me at my desk, I would assume that all of them owned a Wyndham Vacation Ownership with a VIP status, so I thanked them for being VIP Owners. When PCs confessed that they hadn't upgraded to that level of ownership just yet, I responded by saying, "That's okay, I'm sure that you eventually will, even if it doesn't happen today."

I went ahead and treated them like they were already were VIP Owners. I linked their DBVs with VIP benefits. At the end of the presentation, it was usually difficult for the PCs to let go of the concept that they weren't VIPs. They enjoyed the VIP service I provided and couldn't accept that they wouldn't be able to use the benefits that came along with it. At the end of my sales presentations, I gave the PCs three different choices. They often chose to purchase a VIP Ownership.

*You can influence your PC to feel enthusiastic about their choice to buy from you by listening to them, tailoring your presentation to benefit their DBVs, sharing a compelling vision with them, and enabling them to choose to purchase without pressure. When your product or service genuinely connects them with their aspirations—and upholds their Highest Values—you will inspire them to use your product or service to enhance their lives.*

## ADDICTED TO SELF-IMPROVEMENT

I have always stayed away from office gossip like it was the plague. It never proved to be lucrative, nor did it help anyone; it just brought people down.

I was once eating lunch with my coworker on a beautiful, sunny day in Waikiki. She leaned in towards me with a concerned frown on her face. I was a bit confused about what she had to tell me. Maybe she wanted to let me know that I had a piece of lettuce in my teeth or ketchup on my lip. Instead, she sighed and asked, "How do you feel about people saying you are addicted to self-improvement seminars and books?" I laughed and replied, "If that's the worst thing that people are saying about me, then it's a compliment!"

Part of my philosophy in life is to constantly work on getting myself out of my own way and avoid giving into self-sabotage;

THE 60 SECOND SALE

I attribute my career successes and the loving relationships in my life to this ability. However, I had to work hard, take risks, and maintain a laser-like focus to attain this skill. I continuously acquire all the knowledge and experience that I possibly can in order to improve my sales performance and who I am.

For those of us who work in the sales industry, it is vital that we make sure that we are the best version of ourselves at all times. If you find out what makes people tick (especially yourself), you will discover an incredibly valuable life skill. The bottom line is this: you cannot provide a Superb Customer Experience if you are unable to improve how people experience you. Using humanistic methods of selling requires that you have self-awareness and follow the principles of the Circle of Appreciation.

If I am addicted to improving my character and my communication to help myself and others, then I am delighted to honor my addiction. It sure beats being addicted to Sprinkles Cupcakes!

## THE MOST EMPOWERING PHILOSOPHY

Josh was my coworker when I worked at WVO. He would regularly create conflict with his PCs. You could literally predict his progress by how long it took before he started negatively reacting during one of his presentations. If he didn't get a sale or felt that the PCs were being rude in any way, he would lash out at them and be condescending and argumentative. Instead of giving a 45-minute presentation, he would drag it out to 2 or 3 hours. I would hear colleagues sitting near his desk saying, "Oh, there goes Josh again."

He was getting in his own way and bringing misery to his clients and himself. No one wins when there's conflict between the PC and the salesperson.

*The most empowering philosophy is "get yourself out of your own way."*

If you allow things to negatively affect you or distract you from providing Superb Customer Experiences, it will result in you being miserable, broke, desperate for sales, or out of a sales job. Develop consistent strategies that you are committed to, that will enable you to resolve limiting beliefs,[11] and that turn surviving into thriving.

When you learn more about who you are and begin to understand your behavior, you will expand the opportunities in every area of your life. You will get off the sales roller coaster and escape the frustration of the one-hit wonder. Instead, you will experience sustainable sales growth.

Gary Vaynerchuck, a four-time New York Times bestselling author, venture capitalist, and owner of VaynerMedia, says that self-awareness is the most important skill to have. By knowing ourselves we can be proactive in our actions

---

11 Beliefs about oneself that are self-defeating or provide a bleak, dystopian worldview.

and inactions, and ultimately have a better understanding of our PCs personalities.

## ENTRENCHED BELIEFS

You can nip destructive attitudes in the bud by knowing what makes you negatively react or emotionally regress. You can decide now to change beliefs that have held you back in the past. Remember, your beliefs are all in your head; they are not your reality unless you make them so. Only you have the power to change them.

We all create our own reality. If you have the unwavering belief that making $20,000 a month is possible and take progressive action accordingly, then it can become your reality. You must believe that something is possible for it to come to light.

The reverse is also true: you live to prove your beliefs. If your beliefs are limiting you, they will obstruct your progress. Why restrict yourself in this way? You can be right about your entrenched beliefs and be broke, or you can prove your limiting beliefs wrong and become prosperous.

If you can relate to being vulnerable to limiting beliefs and/or to perceptions that inhibit the best version of yourself, set yourself free from them. Recall that since you are working in the service/sales industry, you need to respect and appreciate your employer, your potential clients, and just as importantly, yourself. In chapter 8, I will share a technique that will have you feeling empowered and get your mindset on the right track and on the way to becoming a member of the Sales Elite. This attitude shift will silence your negative beliefs and make way for positive, creative, and inspirational thoughts.

*My addiction to self-improvement has paid off in countless ways.*

Being a top sales performer at WVO, I was blessed to earn several prestigious trips that were paid for by my employer. During them, I stuffed myself with delicious free food, and I got to know the top leaders. I wanted to find out the secrets of their success and the ways to replicate them. I wasn't looking for sales tips; I was more interested in their values, beliefs, and mindsets.

On one of these trips, I entered the resort gym at 6:00 a.m. and I noticed that these leaders were already working up a sweat on the treadmills. I also observed that they left the banquet dinners and parties a little earlier than most of the guests, so I chose to do the same. One of the "really high-ups" shared that he employed a team of personal coaches to support himself by developing his health, mindset, and business. I felt vindicated. Maybe I wasn't alone in being a self-improvement addict!

When I realized that the top leaders at WVO worked on improving their minds and bodies, I felt a boost of confidence and wanted to keep my self-education going.

Today, you're going to make the choice to get yourself out of your own way and provide Superb Customer Experiences.

There's no looking back. Starting now you will start going beyond your PCs' and employer's expectations.

## ACTION STEPS

1. Take a Step Back- reflect on the way your PCs are experiencing your sales presentation. Ask yourself if this is the way you would want to be treated? Are you truly providing Superb Customer Experiences? Know that you can do even better than you already are. Stretch a little more and your Fair Exchange will enable you to take bigger commission checks home.

2. Transform your mindset into being a resource instead of just a salesperson. Assist your PCs to get more of their Highest Values. Implement the strategies to speak directly to their personality type and shift them to express their opposite sides so that they can take bigger leaps into their aspirations of a brighter future.

3. Your sales presentation needs to have the following: fair exchange, bring value, inspiration, empowerment, respect, gratitude, and engagement. Add these elements and work with your manager or supervisor to get their support and guidance.

4. Give value to your PCs even before showing them the features and benefits of your product/service. For example, offer to analyze and organize their personal budget if you're a financial planner or offer to give them a complimentary appointment with an interior designer if you are a realtor on the buyer side.

5. Part of the Circle of Appreciation is to be grateful to yourself. Write a list of 100 reasons why you are grateful

for yourself. Keep this list and re-read it throughout the week. To keep the momentum of feeling confident, powerful, of service, and deserving, read a few items on your list before each of your sales presentations.

6. Do a self-assessment of how you show up for your PCs. You can do this by asking yourself after every sales presentation if you let any personal thoughts, other people's agendas, or poor health choices get in the way of serving your PCs. Without judgement, keep track of the changes and progress you've made in a journal.

7. Every day, challenge yourself to get uncomfortable. Ask questions that you know are valuable to your PCs that you have hesitated to ask in the past. See Key Questions (Chapter 6) for examples.

The Customer Experience Movement needs salespeople like you. You can continue contributing to it by reading books like this one, practicing the exercises laid out throughout this book, and improving how you show-up for your PCs and your employer. Your brand reliability will shine and attract clients and their referrals.

CHAPTER

# 5

# SALES COMMUNICATION AND CONNECTION

*"If you just communicate, you can get by.
But if you communicate skillfully,
you can work miracles."*

~ Jim Rohn

●————————————●

**H**AVE YOU EVER DRIVEN home from work, then couldn't recall your drive after you arrived? You remember getting into the car, and maybe even the first few actions behind the wheel. But upon attempting to recall the actual events of the trip or songs on the radio, you keep drawing a blank.

The first few times that this situation occurs, it can feel scary, but the result is the same: you arrived at home unharmed. Nevertheless, you'll still probably wonder what occurred.

## CONSCIOUS VS. SUBCONSCIOUS

In all likelihood, your subconscious mind took over the task of driving because it knew your commute home routine. It is as if you gave your subconscious mind a command ("drive home"), and your actions were on autopilot. This blank-out occurred while your conscious mind focused on other things, such as dinner plans or your day at the office.

In fact, this situation is usually safer than thinking about every movement. If a car pulls out in front of you, your subconscious mind instinctively reacts and attempts to stop you from crashing. Then your conscious mind kicks in to reassess the situation.

The difference between the conscious and subconscious minds has puzzled experts for hundreds of years, yet studying the mind is not solely beneficial for scientists. In fact, it can be a brilliant pursuit for salespeople. As a member of the Sales Elite, you need to understand the basic differences between the conscious and subconscious minds; it will assist you in understanding your PC's behavior, as well as your own. By knowing which mind to trigger during your sales presentation, you will help your PCs make their purchase decision easier and with less buyer's remorse.

## THE CONSCIOUS MIND

Scientists have estimated that our conscious mind can only process an average of 50 bits of information per second. This might seem like a decent amount of information but not when you consider that our minds can process 11,000,000 bits of information per second.[12]

The conscious mind is responsible for logic, thinking, and short-term memory. It is very important to highlight that the conscious mind tends to focus only on a specific area of decision making and problem-solving at a time, while neglecting other possibilities. Imagine that you are holding a flashlight at nightfall. You turn it on and face the light directly towards the ocean in the dark. The light will only show a small linear view of the ocean, and neglects everything else that is not in that direct line. The conscious mind processes information in a similar manner.

The conscious mind does have a necessary function: It assists you in sorting through incoming information received through any of the five senses. Think of it as your brain's receptionist; it can only answer one call at a time and organizes your messages according to your priorities, deletes useless short-term information, and stores important information in your subconscious mind.

The conscious mind is great at making decisions that are simple and require less processing. If you are selling products

12  George Markowsky, "Information Theory—Physiology," *Encyclopedia Britannica*, 2015

such as hand soaps, towels, and other everyday items that are not complex, then you can rely on your PCs' conscious minds to make quick and concise decisions to make the purchase.

On the other hand, the conscious mind is very poor at making complex decisions because it can only process a small bit of information at a time.[13] There is simply not enough information in the conscious mind to make complex purchasing decisions for items such as life insurance, houses, cars, mortgages, etc. Because it cannot process all of the possible bits of information, your conscious mind "receptionist" simply directs all the noise to "No." Your PCs will feel safer saying "no" if you are either talking only to their conscious mind or telling them too much information. Your PCs will be confused, resistant, and uncertain about becoming your client when they feel bombarded or confused.

Ideally, when you are selling complex items, bypass the conscious mind and get to your PC's subconscious mind. I explain how to do this in the 3 Vital Techniques later in this chapter. This method of communicating will not only maximize the chances of your PCs saying "yes," it will also minimize the possibility of returns and rescissions. Recent studies have shown that consumers are more satisfied with decisions that relied less on the conscious mind and more on the subconscious mind.

---

13 Ap Dijksterhuis, Maarten Bos, Loran Nordgren and Rick van Baaren; "Too Conscious to Decide;" *Kellogg Insight* (Kellogg School of Management at Northwestern University); 2009

The conscious mind is still a vital part of communicating with your PCs. They will need to access this part of their mind when you want them to answer Choice Questions (Chapter 6). When creating a compelling sensory experience, you will also access their conscious minds because our five senses are processed consciously. PCs will also rely on their conscious mind to reject or accept the terms of making the purchase from you.

## THE SUBCONSCIOUS MIND

The subconscious mind is a powerhouse.[14] It processes up to 11 million bits of information every second, controls most of our behavior by acting and reacting, and manages all the information that the conscious mind doesn't find important. Generally, your subconscious mind is the reason why you ate more than your share of chips and salsa while engrossed in your favorite television show or why you're able to drive and talk on your hands-free mobile device at the same time.

The subconscious mind can also handle complex decision making because it stores long term memories and organizes most of our brain's information. You will be communicating to this part of your PC's mind when you explain new concepts, such as why an electric car is better than a gas guzzler or the difference between a government-insured versus conventional home loan.

---

14 Matt James, "Conscious of the Unconscious," *Psychology Today*, 2013

Whereas the conscious mind is easily overwhelmed with too much information, the subconscious mind can handle much more information when that information is communicated effectively. If the conscious mind is like a flashlight on the ocean, the subconscious mind is like a lighthouse when it comes to casting light in the darkness.

Another powerful benefit of the subconscious mind is that it makes associations and learns from experiences. If you were bitten by a dog as a child, your subconscious could trigger your body to send warning signals when it sees dogs. Your heart might beat faster, and your pupils might dilate. On the other hand, if you had warm fuzzy experiences with dogs, then your body could react by reaching your hand out to pet a dog—as if it were a reflex.

Why is it important to understand this concept in sales? If your PCs tell you that they've had a negative sales experience in the past, you need to ask them what happened, and listen to what they share with you. It could be a huge opportunity for you because you will discover what to avoid during your sales presentation. Do the exact opposite of what they consider to be a poor sales presentation. Without knowing the details of their negative experience, you will be unaware of the elephant in the room, which will easily crush your sale.

It is the subconscious mind's ability to store long-term information that makes it a powerful driver of our behavior. When we sense something through our five senses, it is our conscious mind that initially receives that information, but it is our subconscious mind that triggers a memory, experience, or feeling about the information. Smell is a particularly important sense, because it is most highly connected to our long-term memory. Recall that realtors often add clean and warm scented fragrance in the houses they are selling. Their PC's conscious mind smells the scents, but the subconscious mind connects that scent to cleanliness, a new beginning, the warmth of loved ones gathering, and being home.

Last week my husband and I test drove a Tesla Model S at a dealership in San Diego. The salesperson showed us the interior features while we were both seated in the Model S. Had she shown us the features at the sales office through a catalog it would have been more complicated for my husband and I to understand the functions of the features and how to use them. By putting us inside the car while telling us about the features, she was speaking to our subconscious minds. Our subconscious minds were entertained by the beautiful interior, the smell, touching and playing with the display panel, all while having a conversation with the salesperson.

Literally throw everything you've got at your PC's subconscious mind through facilitating a Superb Customer Experience that stimulates as many senses you can apply, communicating to their Highest Values, while showing them the most complex part of your sales presentation.

In addition, the subconscious mind cannot process negative commands because it sees pictures instead of words. For example, let's try out how your subconscious processes directions: Don't think of the color red.

Did you picture the color red? In order for you to process what I'm telling you *not* to see, you had to visualize or otherwise think of the color red. Therefore, a member of the Sales Elite avoids telling their PCs, "Don't worry about the price." If you do, that's exactly what they'll do.

Stacy, the cashier at my local Trader Joe's, was telling me that almost all their clients pull their debit or credit cards out of the machine too soon. I explained to her that it was most likely due to the fact that their machines say, "Don't remove your card." Confused, she replied, "What do you mean?" Then I asked her not to think about a pink ball. Sure enough, she thought about it. Stacy then realized that the credit card machine needed to say, "Leave your card in."

To clarify this concept further, see the negative commands below:

| What You're Saying: | What They Hear: |
| --- | --- |
| Don't worry. | Worry. |
| Don't think about it. | Think about it. |
| Don't shop around. | Shop around. |
| Don't miss this sale. | Miss it. |
| I'm not selling you anything. | I'm trying to sell you something. |
| I'm not like other salespeople. | I'm just like all salespeople. |
| I don't pressure any clients. | I pressure clients. |

*Instead of using negative commands, clearly communicate your intentions:*

### What to Say Instead

- Our clients love how easy and reliable our product/service is.
- What is there to think about?
- I am listening to you to see if our product/service is the right fit for you and your organization/family.
- I specialize in customer service because I enjoy serving people just like you.
- I am here to answer all your questions. If I'm lacking answers, I'll find them for you.
- How can I best assist you today?

It is easy to think that the verbiage you use in sales presentations has little impact on the enrollment. However, PCs' patience and attention spans have decreased. They might hear only a small percentage of what you're saying and remember even less. Because we live in a time where we're trying to do it all, our minds usually toggle from one thought to another. As salespeople, we are constantly attempting to get real estate in our PCs' mind. With such competition for the PCs' attention span, why would any salesperson risk using words that might trigger the effect of negative commands?

Now you are aware that your PCs are more likely to say 'no' to your offer if you only tap into their conscious mind or if you communicate poorly to their subconscious through negative commands or conjuring negative memories. Make an effort to transition them into utilizing their subconscious mind by making positive associations. This concept will make a world of difference in the way you approach the content and context of your sales presentation. This technique enables you to speak directly to who your PCs really are at their core, which gives you a better chance of speaking in accordance with their Highest Values.

By combining the sales experience in their subconscious mind and linking to the data they've stored in their conscious mind, your PC will have a greater chance of answering with a "yes" about purchasing from you.

*Remember, as a member of the Sales Elite who utilizes the 60-Second Sales Method, you only want to spend a small amount of time with a PC's conscious mind.*

To make it easier, use the 80/20 rule. 80% of time, your focus is to gear the conversation to the subconscious mind, and only gear 20% toward the conscious mind.

You can easily adjust your communication style to influence your PCs' emotional state, so that they can quickly decide and feel good about their purchase.

## SENSORY LANGUAGE

Have you ever experienced a time when you attempted to explain how to use a product or the function of an item, only to get a response of utter confusion from your PC? If you answered "yes," you are going to ensure that this situation is avoided by learning and applying the concepts in this part of the chapter.

I am going to take you back to your kindergarten class-room, when your teacher taught you the five senses. It will enable you to speak more clearly to your PC by connecting their sensory preference to your entire sales presentation. No need for flashcards here; you can certainly thank your teacher for showing you one of the most important basics of sales communication.

Everyone tends to favor one or more of the five senses that they use to communicate:

- A *Visual* (seeing) person may say:
  "Look! Can you see the benefits? Just picture yourself...."

- An *Auditory* (hearing) person may say:
  "I hear what you're saying, but that doesn't sound right... Listen..."

- A *Kinesthetic* (feeling) person may say:
  "That feels strange. I'm not comfortable with that. Can we just touch on these other ideas?"

- An *Olfactory* (smelling) person might say:
  "I smell a good weekend is coming up. There's something savory about this bed and breakfast."

- A *Gustatory* (tasting) person might say:
  "I'm hungry for more opportunities. I want to taste success."

Although you interpret the world and your experiences using your five senses, your interpretation of what you feel, hear, taste, smell, and see can get complicated when you take it all in. How you experience your world is filtered by your own past experiences, positive and negative beliefs, thoughts, fears, judgments, values, feelings, and projections. The person next to you would likely experience the same event or setting in a completely different way than you do.

These interpretations influence your sensory language and characteristics. We respond to this world through our perceptions of our experiences. The main point is that we're not all the same; we all speak a unique Sensory Language. Therefore, if you mismatch your language to your PCs' personal communication style, they won't truly understand what you mean. Subsequently, you could waste time clarifying what you say, rather than connecting with your PC. The best communicators can adapt their Sensory Language to suit a wide range of people, and they can quickly assess others' communication preferences.

## EXAMPLES OF SENSORY LANGUAGE

Imagine that you have a PC who has a difficult time visualizing and is more of an auditory communicator. Yet your office is loud, and you keep using words like "see," "picture," and "visualize." You start noticing that you are rapidly losing her interest and focus.

Instead of yelling louder or repeating yourself, take her to a quiet place, and begin to use words such as "listen," "hear," and "sound." The more you allow her to experience your product/service through an auditory experience, the more you will gain her confidence and attention during your presentation.

I am naturally more of a visual person. Since I need to see what I'm selling, I prefer to use visuals: photographs, color charts, and diagrams. At times, I even sketch out what I'm attempting to communicate. As someone who also has an auditory tendency, I need to listen to my PCs. But I've trained myself to be comfortable using all five types of Sensory Language.

We all lean toward our own preferred Sensory Language. It is vital for you to learn which of these languages you prefer to use when communicating, then learn to adapt to the other Sensory Languages. This process will enable you to easily utilize these other languages to better communicate with your PCs. Through your explanations and influence, you will save time and be clearer.

For more examples of sensory words that you would practice using in your sales presentations, see the "Sensory Words" appendices in the back of the book.

## 3 VITAL TECHNIQUES

We've all heard that people tend to like others that are similar to them. In this part of the chapter we are going to cover how you can speak directly to your PCs' subconscious minds.

When eating out at a restaurant, you can easily spot diners that have a good rapport. When you pay a bit more attention, you will begin to notice that their body language mirrors the people they're with, and that they have similar facial expressions. If you listen closely, you might even hear that their tone and verbiage are similar. You can even see that some diners dress similarly.

As salespeople, we would love to have that kind of connection with our PCs right away. However, we might not be able to build that rapport due to one factor: PCs know that they're in a sales presentation. This understanding usually causes them to have more resistance to opening up and being their authentic-self with the salesperson. They want to avoid "being sold."

Therefore, familiarity plays a big role in connecting with PCs. It reminds them that the salesperson is a real person too. In order to achieve the 60-Second Sale, you need to develop this feeling with your PCs as swiftly as possible.

However, building rapport is not as simple as saying, "Hello. Do you like going to the beach? Great! You like the beach, and so do I. You like the Minnesota Vikings? Wow, I do too. We're now best of friends and you trust me 100% with your investments, right?"

Wrong! Just because you have common interests won't mean that your PC is ready to purchase from you. Establishing common interests is merely a way to warm up the new connection, and are so specific that you will only be speaking to your PC's conscious mind. If you recall, only small bits of information can be processed and decided upon at this level.

Nowadays, it is more difficult to quickly bond with PCs because everyone is all-too-familiar with the old "building rapport" sales strategy, so they are skeptical of its use. This is why guiding your PCs' to use their subconscious mind when discussing bigger picture ideas, problem solving, and decision making is necessary.

To communicate with your PC's subconscious mind, begin by first letting go of any tired sales tactics that you might be using, which we covered in the previous chapter. Use genuine interaction, and develop an authentic interest in getting to know your PCs. The challenge is that PCs today lack time to listen to sales presentations, so salespeople feel a sense of panicked urgency to get to the point. Therefore, connecting to a PC on a deeper level is often missed. Yet being patient and investing your attention can make all the difference.

One way to connect with your PC is to genuinely inquire about their interests (Highest Values), learn what's important to them, and ask them "why?" I'll cover how to ask specific questions that you can use during your sales presentations in Chapter 6.

In addition to asking impactful questions, I have discovered three techniques that will assist you in developing swift rapport and enable you to leap into a deeper connection with your PCs. These techniques will enable you to bypass the PCs' resistance and lack of initial interest while speaking to their subconscious mind. These powerful techniques are called: mirroring, pacing, and anchoring.

By following the 3 Vital Techniques laid out below, you can begin to gain trust, a bond, and perhaps a new friend quicker than ever. Have you ever been stuck with PCs that you just couldn't click with, or struggled to find commonalities with them? If you apply these techniques, you can rest assured that these problems will be a thing of the past, since you will be able to connect faster and more easily with any PC.

## 1. MIRRORING

"Mirroring" is the easiest of the three techniques, as you basically act like a mirror of your PC. You reflect their gestures or behaviors. To clarify, if you mimic them like a mime or copy every movement they make, it will come off as rude and creepy. Mirroring is subtler, and if it is done well, it's imperceptible to the PC.

## WHAT DOESN'T WORK
<<WARNING>>

This section is going to break the common beliefs about reading body language that are usually taught in sales books.

A predominant misconception is that you can read body language without verbally communicating with the person. That would mean that you have the superpower of mind reading. If you do, drop this book and head to Las Vegas!

Several of the ridiculous claims I've read include believing that if someone crosses their arms and tightly holds them in front of their body, they're being resistant and standoffish. Do you know how many times I cross my arms because I'm cold?

I once had a PC who exhibited every one of the body language no-no's that you've read about. He had his arms crossed and his hands formed into fists. If I believed traditional sales training, I would have been convinced that he was being extremely resistant, that he didn't trust me, and would not buy from me. However, knowing that his crossed arms reflected nothing about his intention to purchase my product, I continued linking his DBVs and kept engaging his subconscious mind with the prospect of him becoming my newest client. And without any objections, he made a purchase with me.

Another common misconception is that a person's head movements can reveal their true feelings. For example, perhaps a person is saying they like something, but they shake their head left to right several times. If so, the common belief is that their body is revealing that they're lying and that they're actually saying "no" with their head.

From my experience as a facilitator of over 2,000 sales presentations at WVO, I can assure you that this headshake is far from accurate. In fact, sometimes when someone is moving their head from one side to the other, they're actually underlining that statement by using their head. It's as if they're placing several lines under the statement to show their certainty. You also need to keep in mind that body language differs from person to person, as well as from culture to culture.

## WHAT DOES WORK

Certainty is key to becoming a member of the Sales Elite, instead of guessing every step of the sales process. An attempt to read your PC's body language without asking them key questions is a lazy, unreliable way to facilitate your sales presentation. Take the guessing game out of your presentation. Replace it with the time, energy, and care it takes to understand the patterns between an individual PC's body language and what they're verbally sharing with you.

Let's take a look at how to mirror your PCs in subtle and respectful manners. Mirroring allows you to quickly build a rapport because you tend to feel more comfortable with someone you're familiar with. When a salesperson speaks the same sensory language, and uses similar words and body movements, you tend to trust them more.

There are several ways you can effectively mirror someone:

- **With Your Body**
  You can move part of your body to mirror the other person: a crossed leg, a hand gesture, a tilting of the head to one side. You can also mirror their entire posture: slumped body or upright posture.

- **With Your Face**
  You can mirror their facial expressions: a smile, raised eyebrows, puckered lips, and narrowing or widening of the eyes.

- **With Your Voice**
  It can be fun to mirror their volume, speed, rhythm of speech, tone of voice, and even their accents. I have been known to use a slight Southern twang in my pronunciations as needed.

- **With Verbiage**
  Mirror their keywords and phrases. If they speak formally, do the same. If they use a dialect or slang, you could use some similar words (or have a whole conversation using them, if you are fully familiar with the style). That said, if you're not adept at using their phrases, it might be better to avoid this technique, so that you avoid looking as if you're making fun of the way they're speaking.

- **With Breathing**
  Watch the PC's breathing and note if it is through their chest rising or their nostrils flaring. Breathe in the same rhythm, and it will give you a sense of what it is to be at their energy level. At the same time, it will give them the subtle feeling that you are "the same." Use observation, practice, and patience.

When mirroring your PCs, make sure that you do it in a subtle manner. The intention is to communicate to their subconscious mind so that it feels natural for them to engage with you as if you are friends, or at the very least acquaintances, rather than strangers.

## 2. PACING/LEADING

After successfully mirroring, you can now begin to "pace" your PCs to increase rapport with them. Pacing means that you essentially meet your PCs where they are in that moment, and keep the same pace as them: matching their energy, speech tempo, body movements, expressions, or emotions over a short period of time. Imagine that you are jogging with a friend. In order to "keep pace" with your friend, you may need to speed up or slow down. Once you calibrate your own pace, you can begin to match their pace. Eventually, you could slightly alter your pace to run ahead, and then your friend would need to match you. You can also see pacing by watching a group of cyclists on the street or during a race.

The technique of pacing in sales is essentially the same concept: match your style and energy to the PC by altering your own, and once you are comfortable at their pace you can lead them to match yours.

*Remember that the pace that your PC speaks is the pace at which they process information and thoughts.*

The above statement is crucial. If your PC speaks slowly, then they process information slowly. Therefore, if you speak too quickly, you will lose their attention. They will most likely be confused and avoid purchasing from you. The same applies if they speak quickly, so if you speak too slowly, you will lose their interest as well. This concept has nothing to do with their level of intelligence. Rather, it relates to their personality types and the way they process their thoughts. To avoid losing their interest and having them end your sales presentation, make sure that you pace the speed to match their comprehension.

In addition to physical pacing (using the body), you can also verbally pace your PCs' by using similar words, tones, and accent. Review the Sensory Words in the Appendices (back of the book) that matches your PCs' sensory language preference.

Once you have the rhythm of matching your PCs' pace, you can begin to take the lead. Leading means that you start to guide the emotional state, energy level, and the flow of the sales presentation. Just as in the jogging metaphor, pacing requires matching your pace to a target so that you can eventually take the lead in a way that feels seamless.

### Why is leading important?

It's often assumed that salespeople have control of their sales presentation. This is not always the case because PCs can overpower the direction of the sales presentation while leaving the salesperson stumbling behind. These situations occur most often when you are selling to Controllers and Promoters.

### How do you know you're leading?

Test by making small changes in your body posture. You can slightly lean in and see if they lean in too. For example, you can test by showing them a feature of your product or point to a visual reference of your service. If you are leading, then your PCs would lean in as well. Another example: perhaps you've been sitting with your arms crossed for a while in your effort to mirror your PC, then you unfold them. If the PC does too, you are now beginning to lead them.

The intention is to lead your PCs and get them to mirror your movements, energy level, and attitude. This can only happen if you have the patience to build an actual connection with your PC. The goal is to build enough rapport through pacing, being grateful for their time, being a Present Listener, and linking their HVs to your conversations, that they will trust you enough to follow your lead.

The key to leading is to always start by pacing where they are now; I have paced PCs who were initially upset and led them to a state of being happy and excited. I have also led PCs who were not present and distracted to focus and pay attention, which helped them keep the sales presentation on track.

Pacing and leading allows you to turn a negative experience into a positive one without having to cut your prices in half or sell your soul. If your PC is upset, then get upset with them in agreement, instead of resisting and fighting against them. Then as you build rapport by using pacing, lead them into a better state than the one you originally found them in. This technique becomes a win/win situation for all involved.

At one WVO sales presentation, my PCs complained that the resort's daily parking fee was $25 per day. I agreed with them that this amount was expensive, and stated that I had to pay $150 a month to park two blocks away from my office! Then they started to get upset with me about my parking expenses. In addition to relating to them, I decreased their anger, because they empathized with my hefty parking fee. Now that we were all on the same page, I was able to lead them on to other topics and shifted their energy to a more peaceful state of being.

## 3. ANCHORING

Anchoring is a powerful technique that you can use to help improve the mood of your PC, and therefore improve your chance of making the sale. Simply put, anchors are stimuli that bring back a positive memory or feeling. They can be smells, visuals, tastes, touches, or sounds.

THE 60 SECOND SALE

Anchoring is related to the theory of "conditioned response," as demonstrated by Pavlov, the famous behavioral scientist who experimented with dogs.[15] He rang a bell whenever a bowl of food was presented to the dogs, and they would then salivate when they saw the food. After this process was repeated many times, whenever the bell rang, the dogs would salivate—even when no bowl of food was presented. The bell sound had "anchored" good feelings (about food), and even evoked a physical response (salivation) without the food being there. Pavlov called this a "conditioned response."

You can access good feelings about memories and anchor them to other experiences in a similar way. In sales, I regularly use anchors to create states of enthusiasm, and I apply anchors to shift my PCs mood to a positive state of being.

**SAMPLE SCENARIO**

I began by assisting the PC to remember a time when she was happy. To accomplish this goal, I asked her key questions (listed in Chapter 6).

Once I observed that she was at the high point of accessing her happy (state) memory, I applied a simple anchor: a smile reinforced by a physical touch, such as a subtle tap on the wrist, a big smile, and a statement, such as, "Yes, I can relate," or, "Yes, that sounds like fun." During the remainder of the sales presentation, whenever I led the PC to answer

_____

15 Saul McLeod, "Pavlov's Dogs," *Simply Psychology*, 2013

"yes," I would smile and briefly tap her on her wrists, which allowed me to re-access her happy emotional state.

The smile and tap became interchangeable; both were associated with the word "yes" and a positive emotion. They acted like Pavlov's bell and evoked a positive response. Eventually, these anchors become embedded. I could simply smile, and the PC would respond in the positive state I led her to be in.

It is best to anchor at the highest peak of the emotional state you want to have access to. Keep in mind to avoid placing an anchor in their low point.

See the diagram below:

## ANCHOR–A Smile

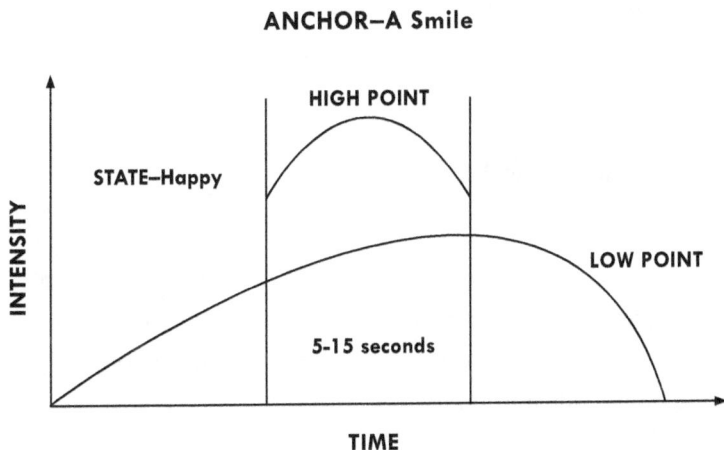

STATE–Happy    HIGH POINT    LOW POINT

INTENSITY

5-15 seconds

TIME

## ACTION STEPS

You are well on your way to understanding that to effectively communicate with your PCs, you need to speak to much more than their conscious mind. It is crucial that you practice these new techniques for communication so that they come naturally to you during your sales presentations and create a more positive Superb Customer Experience for your PCs.

1. Review the Sensory Words listed at the end of the book. Once you are familiar with the words, begin to practice applying them in your conversations. Adjust the Sensory Words to match the sensory preference of the person you are speaking to.

2. Ask someone in your life to tell you something that they've been putting off doing. Then practice the following techniques with them until you enroll them into doing it:
   o Mirroring
   o Pacing/Leading
   o Anchoring

3. As a challenge action step, practice shifting someone's state of being from grumpy or annoyed into a more peaceful or enthusiastic state. Practice these action steps on friends and family members first before attempting them with your PCs.

## YOUR VISUAL BRAND

Have you ever heard of an old saying "a picture is worth a thousand words?" When it comes to achieving your potential as part of the Sales Elite, nothing could be truer. We have mere seconds to make a first impression, so your personal style and actions need to be consistent with the kind of brand you want to create. At all costs, avoid letting your presentation style become an obstacle that you must overcome. Rather, match your style to your personal brand, your industry, your professional image, and the experience you want your PCs to have while they are with you.

Whether you are selling something essential, desirable, or aspirational, your image needs to portray your brand's culture that you want to evoke.

As a Senior Sales Representative at WVO, I had less than 45 minutes to enroll my PCs into purchasing an ownership that ranged from $15,000 to $170,000. I knew I couldn't waste any time or create any more resistance to building a rapport. In fact, I had to earn my PCs' respect and trust within seconds. The instant that a PC looked at me and observed my behavior, I had to be able to convey the following message without speaking a word: "You can trust me. I care about you. I am reliable!"

For ideas and inspiration about how to model myself, I looked at other companies and their "images." What brands did people already trust?

For instance, Nordstrom (a department store) came to mind because they are known for their excellent customer service, and they are a trusted brand that sells high-value luxury goods. Their sales representatives all wear business suits or simple, professional separates that create well-put-together outfits.

I also thought about how teachers present themselves, and how they're well-respected in society. These models provided me with inspiration about how I would dress and present myself. I decided that my attire would be composed of knee-length skirts, paired with simple colored tops (or very minimal prints), and my hair would either be neatly pulled back off my face or styled down. I wanted to look like I took my profession seriously, but I didn't want to be screaming for attention.

Because I didn't wear the latest fashions, nor the laid-back Hawaiian style, I was often the butt of my coworkers' jokes. At one point, I brought an extra skirt to work to get it dry-cleaned. It got into the hands of one of my coworkers, Katy, who was known as the office prankster. She wore my flowered skirt on top of her fitted clothes and pranced around the office as everyone laughed. It was funny to me, but not because she was entertaining.

You see, my coworkers didn't realize that wearing that skirt made me thousands of dollars. I would often get compliments on that skirt from my female PCs, which gave me the opportunity to find a commonality. When your PCs express a similar interest, you have a greater chance of earning their trust and therefore their business.

My PCs at WVO often told me that when they looked around at all the Sales Representatives on the sales floor and saw me, they crossed their fingers that I would be the one allocated to them for their sales presentation. My PCs viewed me as professional because I avoided standing around and chatting with my coworkers. I looked productive, and I gave off a warm, friendly vibe.

The point I am making is this: to make a positive impression and create a quicker connection, you must minimize obstacles and make it easier for your PCs to trust you. In other words, to create trust in your PCs, mirror and model the brands, images, and culture you trust. You never know when a PC is observing you and making a judgment call about you. So look, feel, and act your best at all times.

Your visual brand contributes to the brand reliability that your organization is striving for. Makes sure that your attire and overall impression is a positive representation. It takes only 7 seconds for someone to make a judgement on a first impression (make yours count).[16] This all ties into connecting quickly with your PCs' and insuring that the sales presentation will start off on the right foot.

---

16 Anna Pitts, "You Only Have 7 Seconds to Make a Strong First Impression," *Business Insider*, 2013

THE 60 SECOND SALE

## A BETTER EMOTIONAL STATE

These techniques will enable your PCs to have a fun, positive experience during your sales presentation. When PCs enjoy their sales experience with you, it will be difficult for them to purchase from anyone else. And by representing the culture and impression with your personal brand you will make a great first impression.

Using these techniques in this chapter has enabled me to keep my sales presentations short. This saved time for everyone involved and supported the PCs to leave the presentation at the original time they had expected. Not only will these techniques assist you in keeping track of your time, you will also minimize burning out from attempting to exert too much energy. It will support your PCs to feel comfortable, which will result in a better sales experience for them.

Our responsibility as members of the Sales Elite is to communicate deliberately, which will prevent miscommunication and result in stronger interpersonal relationships with our clients.

Remember, a member of the Sales Elite empowers their PCs to realize their own aspiration; we lead them responsibly through the sales presentations. Regardless of the end result, we leave our PCs and clients in a better state than they originally were in when we first met them.

CHAPTER

# 6

# THE 7 KEY QUESTIONS

*"The quality of your questions*
*determines the quality of your life."*
~ Dr. John Demartini

●————————————●

**M**Y DAUGHTER WAS ONE of my greatest sales coaches. Fortunately, she never went through the "terrible twos" that make some parents cringe, but she was a typical toddler in many ways. Driving home from daycare, our conversation usually consisted of me making a comment, then her asking "why?" Instead of getting frustrated with her repetitive inquiries, I smiled and appreciated my daily lessons.

Thanks to my two-year-old sales coach, I would go into the WVO office the following day prepared. If a PC said, "I don't want to buy," I would ask, "why?" If they answered that question by saying that they didn't take vacations, I would ask "why?" This exchange would continue, and I would discover my PCs' DBVs.

*Asking "why?" is crucial. It allows the PC to express their thoughts, feelings, and beliefs. And more importantly, it allows you to identify their fears, wants, and needs.*

However, asking "why?" is not enough. To speed up your sales presentation, I would encourage you to fine-tune your questions by remembering the following:

- Facilitating sales presentations without asking Key Questions is like shooting arrows while wearing a blindfold.
- Asking insightful questions can trim your sales-presentation time in half, and it will increase your enrollment ratio by 100% or more.

In this chapter, we will explore the 7 Key Types of Questions that will get you reliable results, and we will practice seeing how you can use them to suit your sales presentations. Up to this point of the book, we have covered the essentials that you need to grasp and master the 60-Second Sales Method. In the Introduction, I warned against seeing the 60-Second Sales Method as a get-rich-quick gimmick. As you can see, to master this technique you must do a lot of behind-the-scenes work before you even begin your sales presentation. You have been patient and diligent in getting this far. I promise you that it all comes together soon.

Imagine that we boarded a plane at the very beginning of the book. We have been on the runway gaining momentum with each chapter. You have learned the importance of Fair Exchange and The Circle of Appreciation, how to discover your PCs' Highest Values and the 4 Main Personality Types, the necessity of providing Superb Customer Experiences, and finally how to apply Sensory Language and the 3 Vital Techniques to communicate with your PCs proactively. We are at the edge of the runway, about to lift off into boosting your sales production like never before. The sales techniques that you are about to learn will double, even triple your sales and commissions when you use them consistently.

My intention is to make sure that your journey to becoming a member of The Sales Elite is one that empowers you to thrive in your sales career. Everything that you have learned so far from this book is going to propel you to create a sustainable sales system that you can rely on. Now let's stay on course.

The purposes of asking these Key Questions is to understand your PCs' Highest Values and to have predictable sales outcomes. When you create predictability in your sales presentation, you can better manage the experience you provide to your PCs. Hence, you will yield higher sales conversions and facilitate efficient sales presentations.

## SAMPLE SCENARIO

To illustrate the 7 Key Questions, consider the following situation:

> You're a sales representative with the goal of enrolling potential clients in a grocery-delivery trial membership. You've been assigned to approach people while they are shopping in a particular grocery store.
>
> You spot Jennifer, who's shopping at the grocery store without her family. She's married to Mike, and they have two children. Her time is limited, so you have less than 10 minutes to enroll her in the grocery-delivery membership. You quickly discern that she most likely lives a healthy lifestyle by observing that she has organic produce in her cart.

Let's look at 7 types of questions that you would ask Jennifer.

## 1. CLOSED QUESTION

These questions will often evoke a simple "yes" or "no" answer from the PC. The best way to use this type of question is to start a conversation without appearing intrusive. An intrusive question can easily shut down a conversation before it even starts. Therefore, ask a Closed Question at the beginning of the sales presentation that doesn't ask them to make a purchase.

You can also use Closed Questions throughout your presentation whenever you want to hear a "yes" or "no." Because you risk getting a "no," you need to avoid Closed Questions during the actual enrollment (unless you are completely certain of a "yes.") It's more challenging to find out why they've said "no" to buying your product/service at the end of the process because you have limited time and energy remaining in your negotiations.

> **Examples of Closed Questions:**
>
> "Are these groceries *for you*?"
>
> "*Could* you use more time in a day?"
>
> "*Do* you go grocery shopping every week?"

## 2. OPEN QUESTION

These questions are open-ended because the answers could be anything. The PC could expand on their answer in an unpredictable way. You want your PC to answer this type of question at the beginning of your sales presentation because their answer will give you a starting point for how you will follow-up with other questions. Your PCs and you may be crunched for time, so minimize the amount of Open Questions you ask because they may talk until you've run out of time.

This type of question allows the person to share their values through their answers and is a great way to get the sales presentation rolling. Asking this type of question in the beginning will also give you an insight into how to link your product or service to their DBVs, and it assists you in deciding which other Key Questions to use in the rest of your presentation.

---

**Examples of Open Questions:**

"Jennifer, *what* does feeding your family mean to you?"

"Jennifer, *what* comes to your mind when you think of grocery shopping?

---

## 3. RHETORICAL QUESTION

A Rhetorical Question is a statement in the form of a question. It's probably unrealistic to expect a verbal answer to a Rhetorical Question, because you are stating the obvious. In all likelihood, answers will be in the form of nonverbal agreement.

This type of question is a common way to gain compliance. Now that you have Jennifer's attention, you can launch into your presentation.

---

**Examples of Rhetorical Questions:**

"Doesn't your family *deserve* the *best nutrition*?"

"Wouldn't *saving* money and time be helpful to you?"

---

## 4. INFLUENTIAL QUESTION

In order to influence the answer and the PC's response, this kind of question states a specific point of view in the form of a question. It is meant to predispose the PC to give you the response you are seeking without being overbearing.

---

**Examples of Influential Questions:**

"Healthy groceries can be *very expensive*, but of course you want to feed your family the very best. Do you wish there was a way you could make healthier groceries *more affordable*?"

"Don't traffic and long grocery lines *take valuable time* out of your day?"

---

## 5. CHOICE QUESTION

This type of question empowers the person to answer with the choice closest to their highest value. It gives them a choice, although it is limited to the options you want to offer. Since you can limit the options, you can also decide if you want to keep "no" from being their answer. In other words, the salesperson has more control over the range of answers. However, Choice Questions will naturally minimize the chances of a PC saying "no" because it is just one among several options that *you* decide.

If your PCs can answer all your questions with "no" or "yes," you are using too many Closed Questions and will struggle to enroll your PCs. You need to ask a variety of questions in order to understand their preferences, HVs, and priorities.

By asking them Choice Questions, you can see how they process options and make decisions, especially after you have built rapport.

When you are ready to enroll or ask for the sale, use a Choice Question. Later in the chapter I will give you the Choice Question I often use.

Don, who was not only my sales colleague but a great mentor from WVO, would often ask his PCs a question that gave them 3 options. The first option would be to do nothing (say "no"), and the second and third options involved upgrading their ownership (making a purchase). I thought this technique effectively asked PCs to make direct choices.

One might think that it's crazy to give your PCs the option to say "no." However, I highly recommend that you do because it will reduce the pressure on your PCs from feeling as if they must say "yes." If they take the "no" option, you can always follow up with an Open Question ("why") to learn more and unveil their objections. When asking a Choice Question, offer the choice that you consider best as the last option. It stays in their mind.

---

**Examples of Choice Questions:**

"Jennifer, would you prefer *one free delivery*, or a *30% discount on a one-month membership*?"

"Jennifer, you have 3 options today. One you can say "no" delivery, the 2nd option is a delivery once a week, and the 3rd option is twice a week. Which do you choose?

---

## 6. DIRECTED QUESTION

A Directed Question has a targeted focus on a certain subject area. This type of question leads the conversation in the direction you want it to go. It is a powerful way to shorten conversations and get to the point. It can also assist you to link their DBVs to your product.

> **Examples of Directed Questions:**
>
> What do you *like* about the groceries available in this store?
>
> What *don't you like* about grocery shopping?

## 7. THE 6 WS

To save time with your presentation, be even more specific with your questions. The last category of questions is actually 6 questions in 1, all of which start with the letter "W": What, Why, Who, When, Would, and Will. It's also a review of the 7 Key Types of Questions because it incorporates all of them.

### WHAT

This question digs deeper into the PC's HVs, revealing what is most important to them.

> **Example of a What Question**
> **(also an example of Directed and Choice Questions):**
>
> "*What* is more *valuable* to you: *saving time*, or *spending time* grocery shopping?"

## WHY

This question exposes their values and reveals their higher purpose, which helps you identify their DBV.

> **Example of a Why Question**
> **(also an example of a Directed Question):**
>
> "*Why* is quality food *important* to you?"

## WHO

This question allows you to identify the decision-maker or person of interest, in relation to your subject.

Initially, it is best to ask an Open Question, rather than a Closed Question. (See Example 1 below.)

> **Who Question Example 1 (Open):**
>
> "*Who* is usually responsible for the grocery shopping in your household?"

If you narrow down who the decision-maker is, you'll discover who influences your PC to make the purchase. (See Example 2 below.)

> **Who Question Example 2 (Closed):**
>
> "Are you the person *who* consistently buys the groceries for the household?"

When you want to empower the PC to make a choice, add an Influential Question and Directed Question. (See Example 3 below.)

> **Who Question Example 3 (Influential and Directed):**
>
> "Jennifer, *who* in your family has the *authority* to *make decisions* about a grocery-delivery service?"

And you can even add a Choice Question onto it, such as in Example 4 below. The idea here is that no one normally wants to admit that they lack the "authority" to make decisions in their household.

> **Who Question Example 4 (Choice):**
>
> "Does Mike have the authority to decide or *do you?*

## WHEN

This question will present a timeframe, and more importantly, it will enable you to enroll your PCs right away, rather than later.

Notice that the examples below use Sensory Language. Based on the words your PC uses, respond to them with words from their preferred sensory language.

**Examples of When Questions:**

"*When* can you *see* yourself getting your groceries delivered?"

"*When* do you *feel* that you'll be providing your family with the delivery service?"

"*When* does it *sound* like you'd want to start: today or next Tuesday?"

## WOULD

This question is a gentle way of moving your PC towards enrolling in your product/service.

**Example of a Would Question (also an example of Closed, Influential, Directed, and Rhetorical Questions):**

"*You mentioned* that you and Mike have *busy* schedules. *Would* it be *valuable* for your family to have the household's groceries *delivered* to your home?"

## WILL

This question is forward-thinking and active. It moves the PC towards a committed purchase and time, and predisposes them to select a commitment. It minimizes the pressure to get the PC to commit to a choice and action.

**Example of a Will Question:**

*Will* you be *scheduling your first* grocery delivery this week or next week?

## BONUS QUESTION

This bonus question will reveal how the PC processes their thoughts and actions. This type of question always starts with the word "how."

**How Question Example 1 (also an example of Directed, Influential, and Choice Questions):**

"*How* would you *like* to *settle* the account? Do you *prefer* credit card, check, or cash?"

**How Question Example 2 (also an example of an Influential Question):**

"*How* much time do you think you would *save* per week if you didn't have to go grocery shopping?"

**How Question Example 3 (also an example of a Directed Question):**

"*How* are you going to *use* the extra time that you'll save by having our delivery service?"

## GUARANTEED TO SAVE YOU TIME AND ENERGY

To trim time off from your sales presentations and become proficient in the skills of the Sales Elite, practice asking the 7 Key Questions.

By using these questions, you will:

- Develop a stronger rapport with your PCs.
- Increase your chances of enrolling PCs faster than ever before.
- Gain extra time to increase the number of sales presentations and calls you can finish during your workday.
- Expand opportunities to enroll.
- Double or triple your commission checks
- Improve the livelihood of more clients.

Before you know it, you'll discover that you have gained more free time. By simply applying the 7 Key Questions to your sales presentation, you'll maximize your energy, time, and income.

However, remember to that this set of questions is not a get-rich-quick strategy. Without the following key point of communication, you will certainly fall short:

*You must be a Present Listener.*

Why ask Key Questions if you're not going to listen to the answers? The book starts out with the virtues of listening for a reason. It is the most important part of the process.

*Your PCs will let you know how they want to be enrolled.*

By being a Present Listener and asking clarifying questions, you will be amazed at how quick and easy it is to enroll your PCs. It is imperative that you act as if your PC is the only person in the world when they are talking. Stop getting distracted so easily. Look, a shiny bright object!

Did you look?

In order to maintain your focus, you have to practice. Give your full attention to your PCs. Exclusively focus on them, not your hilarious coworker or your rival's PCs that look more promising.

Here are tips for staying focused on what your PC is saying:

- When a PC is giving you their answers to your questions, mentally block out any noise around you. Ignore your thoughts about your personal agenda. Just be present and listen.
- Their answers provide the key (the "Open Sesame") to what their HVs are. Their words give you useful information, which will then help you link their DBVs to the benefits of what you're selling.
- To identify their DVBs, listen carefully. They're telling you exactly how to enroll them. An impatient salesperson will miss valuable information that the PC is giving them. Remember that part of enhancing the customer experience is to assist them in getting what they want.

- As a member of the Sales Elite, you must understand that your full attention to your PCs is an investment. It's not only lucrative, it's your responsibility.

- Listen with your eyes, as well as your ears. Observe your PCs' body language, gestures, and facial expressions. You are seeking clues about their instinctive, subconscious responses as well as their personality types.

- In Chapter 2, I stated that Newton's third law (every action has an equal and opposite reaction) correlates to the idea that you get back what you give. One of the greatest gifts you can give is being fully present with your PCs when you're listening to them. In exchange, your vision of success will be realized over and over.

- When your PC asks you questions, respond with an encouraging statement:
  - "That's a great question!"
  - "I am glad that you asked!"

- Then follow up with one of the 7 Key Questions:
  - "Why is that important to you?"
  - "What would you prefer?"

When PCs feel appreciated and are more confident about showing their interest, they'll feel more open and receptive to buying because they feel understood.

## ACTION STEPS

- **Create your own examples of the 7 Key Questions.**
  In order to effectively cater to your PCs, you must make these questions relevant to your product or service. You can accomplish this goal through this process:

  - Work through the types of questions one-by-one, in order.
  - Write down the questions you would ask in your own sales presentation.
  - Practice asking them until they become an effortless part of your communication style.

- **Combine two different types of questions.**
  - Make sure you recognize which of the 7 Key Questions you are using, and ask yourself why you are using them in this case.

- **Practice saying the questions aloud.**
  - Make them sound natural.
  - If they lack a natural tone, rewrite them.
  - Incorporate them into your presentation whenever appropriate.

- **Start using the questions with everyone that you talk to.**
  - To make them second nature, start asking these questions in your personal life and not just in your sales presentations.

## MISCOMMUNICATION: A THING OF THE PAST

That would be fantastic, wouldn't it?

The more you use the 7 Key Questions, the greater your focus will be, and the results will amaze you. Your conversations will be more enriched and in sync.

Before you know it, these questions will be part of the way you naturally converse as a member of the Sales Elite. This path leads to saving time and energy, and making certain that you take leaps toward sales success—all the while creating an abundance of free time and energy.

Now that you know 7 different ways to structure questions during your sales presentations, you are ready to put everything you've learned into the 60-Second Sales Method.

The time has come to put your seat in an upright, locked position, and buckle your seatbelt. We're about to take off!

# 7

# THE 60-SECOND
# SALES METHOD

*"Peace does not mean being in a place where there is
no noise, trouble, or hard work. It means being in the midst
of those things and still being calm in your heart."*
~ Unknown

•————————————•

T HE 60-SECOND SALES METHOD will enable you to connect with anyone, even if you're an introvert (or if your PC is). Personally, I'm more of an introvert and prefer to observe conversations than to actually participate in one. If you're like me, then you can rest assured that you'll appreciate this chapter.

However, perhaps you're more of an extrovert, who tends to turn PCs into friends, rather than clients. If so, you'll benefit from reading this chapter as well. The ideal state that you want to achieve is one that both matches the energy of your PCs and mirrors the dominant characteristics of their personalities. But here's the kicker: once you've matched your PCs personality, you can begin to take the lead. Later in this chapter, I will explain this concept in more detail.

*Take this to heart: selling has nothing to do with your own agenda. Instead, it has everything to do with your PC's DBV.*

## THE CHINESE BAMBOO TREE

At the beginning of this book, I could have dived right into the 60-Second Sales Method. However, had I done so, I would have set you up for failure. Let me explain why by sharing a short story. The lessons in this story has helped me be patient, resilient, and persistent, while remaining open to any challenges ahead. It is the story of "The Chinese Bamboo Tree."

In China, there is a type of bamboo that grows like no other tree. When a Chinese Bamboo seed stalk is planted in the ground, it is about 3-4 inches high. During the first year, you won't see any growth in the seed stalk. And during the second, third, and even fourth years, you will notice that the seed stalk is still its original height: 3-4 inches. The tree stays dormant above the ground for the first four years. By the fifth year, the Chinese Bamboo tree exponentially grows up to 90 feet tall, and does so within just 5-6 weeks.

What do you think the Chinese Bamboo tree was doing during the first four years? If you guessed that it was growing below the ground, rather than above it, you are correct. It was settling its roots deep into the soil. In order for the Chinese Bamboo tree to grow to its full, magnificent height of 90 feet, it needs to have strong roots—just like your personal and professional growth. The wind conditions where these bamboo trees grow can be extreme. However, because the bamboo roots are grounded into the soil, the stalks sway effortlessly with the wind. Similarly, your strength, focus, and growth will be tested by unforeseen conditions beyond your control. When you take proactive measures to nourish and prepare your mental state, well-being, and actions, you will begin to expand your potential and achieve new heights.

The sales principles and techniques in this book have enabled you to grow your roots deep into the ground. At times, unforeseen conditions could threaten your foundation and your focus. Like the Chinese Bamboo tree, being flexible about the direction of the wind and having an unwavering determination to succeed will get you through unforeseen conditions.

The sales techniques and principles you have learned in the earlier chapters have been preparing you to apply the 60-Second Sales Method with ease and to have the tools to create a sustainable sales career. You have been settling your roots, let's now discover just how simple it is to quickly transform your PCs into customers.

My first WVO manager and mentor, Terrence, taught me a powerful lesson which I still use to this day. He said, picture a long hallway with doors along both sides of it. All of the doors are open. Your goal is to lead your PC into closing one door at a time through genuinely connecting with them and leading them to link your product/service with their DBVs. If you skip one door, your PC could slip through that opening and miss the opportunity to benefit from your product/service, and you will be out of a client.

The idea is to utilize the 60-Second Sales Method *through-out* your entire presentation. Think of the doors in the hallway as representing each of the fears, resistance, and objections your PCs have. You're going step-by-step, leading them to close one door at a time by answering their questions and by providing Superb Customer Experiences where they trust and decide to become your client. Before we dive into the steps of the 60-Second Sales Method, we are going to cover an important pre-step that is required for you to succeed.

## PREPARE

*Before you start any sales presentation, you must first prepare your energy and mindset.*

### GET GROUNDED

Without this pre-step, you will be starting on a shaky foundation. Grounding yourself enables you to be ready for any PC's personality, objections, and other conditions that could hinder your sales presentation. Additionally, it will enable you to have a clearer purpose and laser-like focus. When you invest time in organizing your mental and physical space, you are declaring to the world: "I'm open for business!"

- **Shake It Off**

    Taylor Swift is probably onto something. Before walking into a room to meet your PCs, you can literally shake off negative energy that you might be feeling.

    This exercise has been utilized by actors and yoga practitioners for many years. They literally shake each part of their body to rid themselves of negative energy. Then, they can re-focus and be ready for what's ahead. It's as if they're shaking off a dark cloud that's hovering over their body.

    You can "shake it off" in a private setting—anywhere away from nosy coworkers. Start with your arms, then your torso, and end with your legs. Be gentle and have fun with this technique. It can provide a great physical and mental signal that it's time for you to get focused and shift energy.

    If you can't "shake it off" in your office, imagine yourself removing any emotional baggage or negative feelings. Feel fresh, present, and gaze at the opportunities ahead. Then clap or rub your hands together, so that you can feel and hear that you've shifted to a more positive mood.

- **Practice Stillness**

  After you've shaken off negativity, get yourself into a space of stillness and peace through the following practices:

  ○ Imagine that you've placed all of your worries and concerns into a black duffle bag. See yourself zipping up the bag and leaving it at the front door of your office. This idea may sound silly or, for some, outrageous. It was a career savior for me when I was weathering through my divorce and much more in 2006. You're not getting rid of your personal or professional issues by any means. Rather, you're just putting them aside so that you can focus on your PCs without distractions. Once you are done for the day, you can easily visualize picking up your black bag on your way out of the sales office.

  ○ Take time to write a gratitude list of at least 20 things, people, or experiences that you're grateful for. If you're absolutely strapped for time, make your gratitude list in your head, and select 5 items, instead of 20.

  Take the time to really *feel* (as opposed to just think about) the items on your gratitude list. When you feel the warmth and joy of the events or people you listed in your gratitude list, you will be a magnet for positive vibes throughout your day. (For example, really *feel* the love for your child or partner. Really *feel* the happiness from when you last laughed out loud or felt loved or appreciated.)

**EMBODY THE CHARACTER**

The quickest way to lead someone into a state of being is to get yourself into that state first.

If your sales presentation is meant to evoke a fun experience, go back to a time in your life when you had fun. Picture yourself at that exact time: laughing, feeling great, and being full of high energy. Your energy level will be higher and enthusiastic, which will be demonstrated by your being, body posture, your movements, and your tone of voice. You will be genuinely embodying exactly the fun experience you want your PCs to enjoy.

However, if you need to be in a serious, professional state, go back to a time when you accomplished a very important task or were recognized for being a great leader.

The process of embodying the character triggers your subconscious to bring those events from your memory back to the present and will cause your attitude, body language, and energy to match those memories.

**BONUS TIP**

If you are normally very nervous when approaching strangers, just remember that they are likely feeling the same as you. We sometimes tend to put others on a pedestal and see ourselves as separate—perhaps unworthy of their business, friendship, or connections. This thinking is false. It's simply fear of the unknown.

*F.E.A.R. stands for False Experience Appearing Real.*[17]

Here is the process for preparing to close the doors in that hallway. Follow the simple, but powerful steps below and continue to repeat them throughout your sales presentations.

## THE 60-SECOND SALES METHOD

## STEP 1: CONNECT

From the instant you meet your PC, you can begin assessing which of the 4 Main Personality Types they are. Take the first few seconds to greet your PC and establish a friendly introduction.

### A. THE HANDSHAKE

When you meet your PC, let her lead you into discovering the most dominant quadrant of her personality. Refer back to Chapter 3 for a refresher on the many ways you can spot the different personality types. However, an instantaneous clue is the handshake. You will get hints from the moment she shakes your hand:

- Is it a strong, gripping-like handshake with direct, almost challenging eye contact? If so, you're most likely meeting a Controller.

---

17 My mentor, Richard, taught me this acronym.

- Is it simply a firm handshake with some direct eye contact? If so, it probably means you've met an Analyst.
- Is it a high five, or a long, enthusiastic handshake with bouncy eye movements? If so, the PC could be a Promoter.
- Is it a tender handshake with slight-to-no eye contact? If so, you're most likely meeting a Supporter.

Use these hints to determine how you approach the next part of your sales presentation.

### B. WARM REGARDS

Regard your PC as warmly as you would your oldest, dearest friend. That might seem like a tall order, but work your way up to this attitude before you even speak to them. At first, find something that you like about them. Do you like their smile, their energy, or their attire?

Observe the ways that a PC reminds you of someone that you know and already feel comfortable with. At this stage, it doesn't matter if they're truly similar to someone you know, it's the positive energy you exude that's important.

Notice the similarities, no matter how small or insignificant they may seem. They will create a warm connection and foster a genuine rapport.

## STEP 2: MIRROR, PACE, THEN LEAD

Start the conversation with your PC by asking Closed and Open questions to get them talking. Listen with your ears and eyes by observing their body language, their preferred sensory language, and energy level. Add clarifying questions as follow-ups to your Closed and Open Questions.

Begin to mirror their words, energy, and body language. Once you are mirroring all three comfortably, you will be simultaneously pacing them as well.

Whenever a PC responds in the way you want them to, begin anchoring a good feeling with a smile, a nod, a keyword, or a light respectful touch (or all three depending on your sales presentation context).

At this point, test if you can take the lead by seeing if they will mirror your movements. You can do one or all of the following: lean in, lean back, smile, raise your voice, lower your voice, and any other small body movement that your PC can follow easily.

You will apply this step throughout your entire sales presentation. Remember that the connection must be continuously nurtured, so you will need to be sure to maintain it by mirroring, pacing, and leading throughout the presentation.

## STEP 3: ASK, LISTEN, THEN LINK

Your goal is to be enrolling your PC throughout your entire sales presentation by appreciating her, giving her a Superb Customer Experience, and connecting your product or service to her HVs. To enroll PCs throughout a presentation is to guide them to close one door at a time—by asking questions, listening to their answers, then directing them to your product or service in a genuine way. It's important that you enroll in small doses. This prevents your PC from feeling pressure or annoyance.

You've already asked your PC Closed and Open questions to get them talking (so that you could mirror, pace, and lead them). As your PC answers your questions, ask clarifying questions that incorporate the 6 Ws. The point of these questions is not to jump right into enrolling the PC, it is to discover her HVs. Continue this process and adjust the Key Questions you ask until you are very clear about what her Highest Values are.

Recall that your PC must be doing most of the talking. You speak 20% and she speaks 80%. I cannot adequately stress the importance of listening to your PC. This is why you will devote most of the time during your sales presentation to being a Present Listener.

After you have listened to your PC's answers, clarified using further questions, and discerned her Highest Values, it is time to start linking your product or service to her DBVs. To do this, start by asking questions that highlight a disconnect between her DBVs and her current situation. Then, offer your product or service as a solution that will improve her life.

- Ask a Rhetorical Question to get an agreement with your PC.
- Ask an Influential Question to prove that you understand your PC.
- Ask a Directed Question to save time and get to the point.
- Ask a couple of Choice Questions to narrow down her preferences and options.

At this point, your conversation will be entirely centered on your PC. You have demonstrated that you understand and appreciate who she is as a person and the kind of life she wants for herself. By linking your product or service to her DBVs, you have led her down the hallway and she has closed one door at a time.

## STEP 4: THE LAST DOOR

When your sales presentation is nearing the end, it is time to enroll your PC with asking a Choice Question that will give her the opportunity to become your client. This is considered *assuming the sale*. The benefit of applying the 60-Second Sales Method throughout your entire sales presentation is that you will be continuously enrolling your PC. Therefore, you will not need to be *closing* the sale at the end, because you've been enrolling your PC all along.

There's only one door left. Now *assume the sale* by giving your PC choices.

Give her no more than 3 choices:

- Choice 1: Do nothing/say no
- Choice 2: Yes (the option that is perfect for her)
- Choice 3: Yes (the option that is above what she wants)

If your PC chooses *Choice 1*, first reassure her with some kind of agreement, such as by saying "That's okay," or, "I understand." Doing so reinforces your connection and keeps you pacing with her. Then, follow-up with an Open Question to clarify the reason behind her answer. It is important to avoid arguing or disagreeing with your PC, because doing so will only distance you from her. Instead, be in agreement with her decision. Then, you can repeat Steps 2, 3, and 4 again.

In most cases, your sales presentation will be longer than 60 seconds. Therefore, you will need to do steps 2 and 3 throughout your entire presentation. Keep repeating Steps 2 and 3 until you are ready to enroll. Then repeat step 4 and ask an enrollment question once you know you're ready to *close the last door*.

## THE 60 SECONDS THAT MATTER

Have you ever heard that the most important part of a basketball game is the last three minutes? While the entire game is a preface for these final moments, many viewers are mainly interested in the exciting conclusion. Similarly, any sporting event really comes down to a series of crucial moments, these are the "highlight" moments you see on

*SportsCenter.* The game may have taken three hours, but the team spent years practicing, and the crucial moments in the game may add up to only a few minutes.

The same is true for sales. While it may likely take you longer than the last 60 seconds to enroll a PC into a client, the majority of the enrollment occurs during your prep work and during the process of listening to your PC. Additionally, the crucial seconds during your presentation, the ones that actually result in enrolling a new client, add up to just one minute.

Therefore, I have broken down the four steps into the number of seconds that they will take to implement once you have practiced and perfected the 60-Second Sales Method. Now that I have fully implemented this method into my sales system, I am able to work through these steps in just one minute.

### CONNECT IN 5 SECONDS
I start every sales presentation with a handshake (to assess my PC's personality type), a smile and friendly attitude (to make a strong impression) and a genuine interest and care (to establish warm regards).

### MIRROR, PACE, THEN LEAD IN 5 SECONDS
I mirror my PCs from the moment I meet them. Most often, I will mirror their facial expression, energy, body posture, and tone of voice.

I continue to do this until I know I've matched their pace. Then, I start to lead them towards the energy I want them to have. Though this may initially just take a few seconds, the reality is that I am engaged with this step continually throughout my presentation.

### ASK, LISTEN, THEN LINK IN 40 SECONDS

The key questions that I ask PCs only take a few seconds each. Since my PCs do 80% of the talking, I keep my questions brief. That way, I can devote more time to listening to my PCs' answers. For the majority of this time I will be listening, and linking my PCs' DBVs to my product or service.

I understand that this may sound counterintuitive because we're talking about seconds here. Trust that being a Present Listener will ultimately save you time, yield sales, and loyal clients.

### CLOSE THE LAST DOOR IN 10 SECONDS

This last step only takes 10 seconds because I have been enrolling my PCs, one door at a time, throughout my presentation. I offer my PCs a choice that minimizes the pressure to say "yes" and allows them to walk through the final door themselves.

*Overall, meet a PC where they are, build rapport, understand them, and take them along with you. You are now providing a Superb Customer Experience for your PCs by being a resource and helping them get what they want (they will be grateful for it). You can expect to receive fair exchanges in mutual respect, new clients, and a thriving sustainable sales career.*

## PRACTICE THE METHOD

It is imperative that you practice the 60-Second Sales Method with your coworkers, friends, and family before you attempt it with Potential Clients and before you can complete all 5 steps in just 60 seconds.

The 60-Second Sales Method will not come easily or quickly. Like Kobe Bryant, you must practice, stay focused, and gain sweat equity.

Before you know it, the 60-Second Sales Method will automatically create segments of your entire sales presentation. Remember, you are constantly enrolling your PCs. The goal is to ask Key Questions until you discover the PC's HVs, then link their DBVs to your product/service, and ask for their business.

Rather than closing a deal, you are simply getting your PC to close one door at a time. Then the only door left for your PC to go through is the one you've provided for them as your newest client.

# 8

# DAILY SALES ACTIVITIES

*"Nothing is impossible,*
*the word itself says, 'I'm possible.'"*
~ Audrey Hepburn

●———————————●

T O  B E G I N  Y O U R  J O U R N E Y  of becoming a member
of the Sales Elite, follow these simple steps on a daily
basis. If you have been studying the concepts in this book
and have begun applying them in your sales presentation,
then you are already committing yourself to putting what
you've learned into productive use.

Just reading this book alone isn't enough to experience all
the benefits that the sales techniques, principles, and methods would give you, your clients, and employer. Test them
all for at least 90 days and see how your sales presentations
become shorter and more efficient with higher conversions.

By consistently applying the 60-Sales Method, you will continue to enhance your sales expertise and send your sales career and commissions into the stratosphere.

I have already detailed the most important practices that have allowed me to sustainably apply the 60-Second Sales Method. The more you become an expert at applying the sales techniques and embody the principles of the 60-Second Sale, the more it will become part of your instinctive behavior.

Implement these final action steps into your daily routines and you will soon be in awe of your extraordinary accomplishments. You will be empowered to enroll PCs into your clients faster while providing them Superb Customer Experiences. You will gain more time and reserve your energy for the things and people that matter most to you. Sounds amazing, doesn't it? Once you begin this new journey with clarity and vision, you will see how bright your future truly looks.

## VISUALIZE TO MATERIALIZE
Visualization is one of my most powerful secrets for supporting my sales production. We have an average of 60,000-80,000 thoughts a day. Most of my thoughts in 2004 were unproductive and random, and I realized that I had to change them if I was going to revise my status as a financially broke, uninspired person.

In other words, I needed to become aware of what I fed my mind. I discovered visualization and since then, I've been applying this method—in conjunction with sweat equity—to turn my visions into a reality.

Visualization can help you unite your subconscious and conscious minds. Our creativity, intuition, and emotional state are all found deep within our minds and hearts. We can work to develop those areas through visualization, meditation, and creativity.

## SAMPLE SCENARIO

A study conducted by Russian scientists compared four groups of Olympic Athletes prior to the 1980 Games.[18] Group 1 did 100% physical training. Group 2 did 75% physical and 25% mental training. Group 3 did 50/50, and Group 4 did 25% physical and 75% mental. The scientists concluded that Group 4 performed the best during the Olympics. How was that possible? You might be surprised to learn that brain scans showed that mental training stimulated the same regions of the brain as the physical training.

This study proves that investing energy in visualization will create tangible, measurable, desirable results. Putting effort into our mental state and emotions requires taking control of what goes on in our hearts and minds, and it affects the outcomes we get.

18 Sarah Schmalbruch, "Here's the Trick Olympic Athletes Use to Achieve Their Goals," *Business Insider*, 2015

Our mindset along with our actions yields results. When your state of mind and skills support you to work with purpose, discipline, and dedication, you will see the results in higher sales production. And the results you'll see are increases in enrolling PCs into loyal clients and an increase in your commissions. Starting today, begin feeding your mind thoughts and visualizations that are healthy to your sales career.

---

## YOU'RE THE STAR OF THE SHOW

Visualize yourself achieving your dreams and goals and being a member of The Sales Elite. Feel, hear, see, smell, and taste your bright vision of a prosperous sales career.

You are now watching a play. The story displays that the character is enrolling one client after another and getting feedback that they are happy with their purchase. In fact, everything that you want to occur in your sales career is acted out in this story.

And then you realize that the star of the show looks familiar. In fact, it's you! You've been watching yourself experiencing the sales career you want to have.

All accomplishments and innovations begin in the mind first.

## MEDITATE TO CULTIVATE

For beginners, meditation may feel like a daunting ritual, but it is definitely worth your time and patience.

Experiment with different methods of meditation. If one way doesn't work for you, use another technique. Do the type of meditation that suits you best. There's no right or wrong way of calming your mind. Remember that there is more value in taking action than not taking any action at all.

For example, I discovered that I am not great at meditating while I am sitting down. My limit is 15 minutes max. I get restless. But that unwanted result didn't cause me to give up on meditation. Instead, I have found that walking in nature, taking salt baths, and reading spiritual books gives me peace of mind and tranquility.

Here are examples of meditation that you may not have considered:

- **Walking**
  Take a meditative walk outdoors. Let your senses absorb the wonders of nature and you'll feel grateful for the beauty that surrounds along your path.

- **Repetitive or Physical Activity**
  Many people find that ironing clothes, preparing meals, and doing other household tasks can be meditative. Remember "monkey brain" from Chapter 2? If you are absorbed in the moment in a multisensory way during

"mindful meditation," it helps empty the mind of nagging anxieties that interfere with clear thinking.

- **Swimming and Bathing**
  You can meditate in the water by swimming in the ocean or a river. When I lived in Honolulu, every day after work, rain or shine, I would immerse myself in the ocean at Kaimana Beach for at least 15 minutes. I visualized that I was releasing negative energy while reconnecting to the abundance of the earth and the universe.

  I now soak in salt baths several times a week. These baths are known to release toxins and negative "gunk" and revitalize the skin, mind, and aura. If anything, your skin and muscles will thank you for pampering them.

- **Listening to Meditative Audio**
  If you have trouble visualizing or focusing on meditation, you may prefer to use audibly led meditations. Guided meditations and visualizations can utilize both narration and music. This sort of meditation is helpful if your mind tends to drift. It helps bring your attention back to the words or music, so you can let everything else go.

  When you listen to guided meditation or music, keep in mind that certain sounds are more conducive to enhancing the brainwaves you're seeking. There are five different types of brainwaves that have been identified in the human brain, which impact your state of being. They all occur naturally, in certain states (such as deep sleep or excitement). They can also be stimulated through certain pieces of music or orchestrated sounds.

For example, Mozart is said to be good for listening while learning, since the beats in his music mimic and encourage theta brainwaves. If you listen to sounds or music that do not match the state of mind you want to create, your meditation practice could be hindered.

Here are the five types of brainwaves:

1. **Alpha Waves** induce relaxation and help reduce stress.
2. **Beta Waves** enhance motivation and alertness and increase energy. While excitement is good, avoid too much Beta Wave activity, because over exposure to it can also cause stress and anxiety.
3. **Gamma Waves** increase memory and heighten the perceptions of all five senses.
4. **Delta Waves** are the slowest of the waves and enable deep sleep.
5. **Theta Waves** heighten emotional awareness, learning, and creativity, and they create a good state for learning and taking in information.

Now more than ever, it's easier to listen to music that can activate certain brainwave activities. You can download the music through smartphone apps, such as Pandora, iTunes, and Spotify. If you are just learning how to meditate, search for Alpha Wave meditation music.

## EYES ON THE PRIZE

Remember the Daily Gratitude Exercise from Chapter 1? One of my most valuable possessions is sitting on my nightstand: my first Gratitude Journal. When I started writing in it, I didn't realize the miracles that my writing would catalyze.

I started writing in my journal in 2006. One of my first entries was: "I am grateful now that I have $50,000 in my bank account." I initially felt a pang of doubt about this figure. At that time, I had less than a $2,000 in my checking account. But I knew that unless my feelings and beliefs aligned with my words, my goal would not become my reality.

I got out of my own way and truly concentrated on feeling, hearing, and seeing what it would be like to have $50,000 in my bank account. I applied the sales techniques, principles, daily activities, and the 60-Second Sales Method every day, and before long, my bank account reflected that amount. The energy of my mental belief—and my emotional connection with my sweat equity—turned my goal into a reality.

Next, I broke down my goals into chunks: Instead of focusing on selling $100,000 per month, I focused on $10,000 per week. Once I achieved that weekly goal, I increased it to $15,000, and kept incrementally increasing it from there.

At the end of each calendar year, WVO presented a highly sought-after award to their top producers at a ceremony called the President's Club. In 2006, I found out that the next President's Club Awards Ceremony was being hosted in a resort I'd wanted to visit ever since I was a teenager: the Atlantis Resort in the Bahamas.

Despite my financial success, 2006 was a challenging year for me. During that one year:

- I started working in the Vacation Ownership industry (an industry with a steep learning curve).
- I was going through a divorce.
- I had to share custody of my 4-year-old daughter with my ex-husband.
- My biological mother passed away before I got the chance to reconnect with her.
- My new company shuffled me through 6 different managers within that one year.
- It rained for 30 days straight in Oahu, which caused 48 million gallons of raw sewage to spill into the waters of Waikiki Beach. I'd finally earned a desk with a 180° view of this famous beach, and now the view was a mile full of brown sewage water. Warning signs replaced the normal crowds of people enjoying the beach.

What were my chances of earning the prestigious President's Club Award after my first year in my new profession? Zero, but it was at the Atlantis Resort! It was the very destination I'd dreamed of visiting since I was a teenager. I'd always longed to speed down the transparent waterslide, which had real sharks swimming around its tunnel. It looked incredible, and it had been an unrealizable goal for many years. And now, here was a real opportunity to make that dream come true. I had to make it; this was my chance.

I took home the President's Club booklet, with its colorful images of the Atlantis Resort and its amazing amenities. Every day after my dip in the ocean, I would go home and open the booklet, drinking it all in. I would visualize what it felt like to be walking through the front door of the resort, the spring of its thick carpet beneath my feet. I visualized the grand lobby's main staircase and felt the cold touch of the metal handrail under my fingers. I "heard" my name being called out as a President's Club Award winner, "listened" to everyone applauding, and "saw" their beaming smiles. I thought it, felt it, heard it, saw it, lived it, and believed it.

November 2006 was the last month I had left to achieve the total sum of $1.2 million in sales for the year, which would enable me to attend the President's Club at Atlantis Resort.

The previous month, I was supposed to have been promoted to the In-House Sales department. However, because of internal issues with another sales representative, I was overlooked. I justifiably could have gotten angry and complained, insisting that I was owed that promotion based on my sales production and work habits. However, I focused on achieving the President's Club award.

Finally, on December 1, 2006, I received the news that I had been officially promoted to the In-House Sales department, and I had achieved $1.3 million in sales! I had earned the President's Club award. My dream of sliding down that famous shark slide would become a reality.

Three months later, I was lying on the private beach of Atlantis Resort and sipping the best piña colada I've ever had in my life. I had finally proven to myself that with sweat equity, discipline, focus, gratitude, and visualization, I had the power to create the sales career I wanted.

## THE LAW OF ATTRACTION

In January 2007, I challenged my mindset and relied on the visualization principle again. At this point in my life, I became a true believer in the Law of Attraction. I was originally introduced to this concept when *The Secret* documentary was released in 2006. I made a commitment to watch *The Secret* every day for 30 days in order to test the concept. The results were astounding. I became a magnet for more qualified PCs that converted to loyal clients, I experienced more opportunities that supported my Highest Values, and I became more confident to stretch my goals.

Many viewers who saw The Secret, rejected the concept of The Law of Attraction because it seemed too bogus and mystical, while others like myself felt that it had truth and applied it in our lives. I find that in order to learn, grow, and improve my sales expertise, I prefer to test concepts and techniques instead of making judgements without personal experience.

THE 60 SECOND SALE

The Law of Attraction has scientific evidence to show how it works. In a simplified explanation, the brain region that is activated with intention also effects the brain region that controls actions. Therefore, having clear intentions drives us to take action. However, our intentions have to be unwavering and without any doubt for our actions to be activated.[19] This could by why salespeople who are positive and optimistic about every situation also tend to attract their vision of being successful in their sales career.

Be aware that the Law of Attraction requires more than just wishful thinking. It needs your actions and perseverance to work. Avoid assuming that it works like a genie in a bottle, who would magically make all of your wishes come true. Think of it more as an accelerator for manifesting your intentions. You need to take actions and be committed and disciplined in achieving your goals. The reality is that we are already practicing the Law of Attraction subconsciously every day. The difference is that we must be conscious about applying it and be specific in our intentions.

In 2007, I printed a fake blank check from a template I found online. In the "to" section, I wrote my full name, and in the "from" section, I wrote "The Universe." The amount to be paid was the sum of $500,000, and I dated it 12/31/2007.

I pinned this check on my fridge at eye level and looked at it every day. Every time I went to open the fridge, I kept

---

19 Srinivasan Pillay, "Is There Scientific Evidence for the "'Law of Attraction'," *Huffington Post*, 2011

imprinting the image of that check in my mind. I visualized the experiences it would allow me to enjoy, and the positive effects it would have on my daughter, my other loved ones, my PCs, and my employers. I visualized everything I wanted to do with that income.

At the beginning of 2008, I received my W2 for 2007. I looked at my earnings for that year, which showed $498,201.24. I certainly wasn't complaining that it wasn't exactly $500,000!

*Keep in mind: I didn't earn this income through just wishful thinking and only visualization. As I have already shared and will clarify again, it took sweat equity, investment in my self-education and self-development, discipline, and an unwavering intention to manifest this goal.*

I have spent the last 10 years studying top sales producers, business leaders, and mega-entrepreneurs. They practice the following: positivity, hard work, appreciation, self-mastery, the Law of Attraction, and clear intentions.

*When you structure your goal to suit your milestones, you'll be able to discover opportunities that you didn't know existed.*

To apply the Law of Attraction, follow these steps:

1. Do the Gratitude Journal exercise every day or every evening. You will need to be in a space of gratitude and peace to get started and to keep the momentum.

2. Be clear on your intentions. In your Gratitude Journal, you write what you would like to have and experience as if it already happened. These statements are your intentions. Make sure that you write a date to when you want those statements to be manifested.

3. Use as many of your 5 senses to supercharge the intentions you write in your Gratitude Journal. For example, if you want to visit Italy visualize eating at Italian restaurants as often as you can or go eat at one in your neighborhood. Visualize yourself sipping an espresso in Rome, hearing the mopeds bustling on the cobblestone streets. Visualize yourself already in Italy.

4. Visualize to Materialize. Take a moment every day or evening to visualize your intentions. See and feel them becoming a reality.

5. Take action steps. Work diligently towards the goals/intentions you have written in your Gratitude Journal, be open to new opportunities, and take action when they present themselves.

Knowing how to magnify your potential and applying these methods to your daily routine are keys to channeling your energy and time. The Law of Attraction supercharges your efforts and assists you in getting to your destination faster. You'll experience going from the slow lane to the racetrack, passing go every time.

## YOUR HOURLY NET WORTH

My WVO coworkers were in awe and disappointed when I decline joining them for Happy Hour after work. I was extremely disciplined, mainly due to one factor: my Hourly Net Worth. It was very easy to analyze my priorities when I knew what was at stake.

You see, I imagined that my sales experience at WVO was partially a work lab. There, I tested all sorts of greetings and enrollment processes. I even tested how my body responded to the way I fueled it, and how that related to the way I facilitated my sales presentations.

### PROACTIVE MEASURES

Here are valuable tips about how to be proactive with your health and mental state.

*Show up to work after having at least 7 hours of sleep.*
Your body will tell you how many hours of sleep it needs, so listen to it. I noticed that whenever I had less than 8 hours of sleep, I wouldn't be at my best and my sales presentations would be off track.

*Eat a healthy breakfast consisting of foods that fuel your brain.*
Certain foods send your digestive system into overdrive and take energy away from your brain. You make it more challenging to provide a Superb Customer Experience if you are in a food coma.

When you eat breakfast or lunch during your work days, choose a light meal. Skip eating heavy, greasy, and gassy food. When you are at a breakfast or lunch meeting with your sales team, avoid being tempted to eat a big fat steak or syrup-covered French toast with bacon and sausage. You might think that because you're getting a free meal, you need to take advantage and order the biggest entrées. I'm all about you taking advantage of a free meal, but not at the cost of your sales performance.

Avoid being the one burping up your meal at your next sales presentation. Prioritize an alert mental state, instead of a belly that's busy digesting a stack of pancakes or a burger.

### *Avoid alcoholic beverages the day before your sales presentations.*
I also noticed that if I had even one glass of wine the night before I had to work, it would throw off my sales process.

I am a light drinker. Alcohol affects me just as much as caffeine does. Just a few sips and the effects are magnified. As much as I enjoy a couple of glasses of Pinot Noir, I avoid drinking the night before I work or attend a networking event.

### HOURLY NET WORTH FORMULA
The Analyst side of me had to break down how one glass of wine would affect me. I was able to figure it out by using the Hourly Net Worth Formula.

This formula enables salespeople who are paid on commission to pinpoint their hourly pay.

First, multiply the total hours of work in a week by the total weeks of work in a year, which will create your total hours in a year. Then, determine your annual income by adding together your commission, bonuses and base pay. Next, divide your annual income by your total hours per year. Then you will see your Hourly Net Worth.

For instance, the formula below assumes that I work 5 shifts of 6 hours apiece every week, take two weeks of vacation per year, and make $300k per year

30 hours X 50 weeks = 1,500 hours. $300,000 divided by 1,500 hours = $200/hour.

*According to this formula, my Hourly Net Worth is $200.00 per hour.*

Let's use my Hourly Net Worth to find out how much one glass of wine ultimately cost me:

One glass of wine = $15 (That's the price at a restaurant in Hawaii. I know, it's steep!)

Time spent enjoying the wine = 1 hour (I'm a slow sipper.)

Work hours impacted by the glass of wine = 6 hours (Total work hours in one day.)

Since my Hourly Net Worth is $200/hour: $200 x 6=$1200

The total cost of the wine = $1,215 (includes the cost of the wine.)

Now you can easily see why it wasn't hard for me to skip Happy Hour and head home to recharge. If you have a hard time saying "no" to opportunities that may not serve your sales career, then use the Hourly Net Worth Formula to assist you. It is a helpful way to see the monetary value of your actions.

At this point, you might think that I am the fun police. I do want you to have fun, just not at the expense of achieving your sales goals or sabotaging a thriving sustainable sales career. Instead, do activities that really recharge and relax you (and therefore add value to your time). You need to be at your very best to be able to apply the 60-Second Sales Method. Do an inventory of your daily activities and move those that hinder your progress to your weekends.

Note that if you are unemployed, earning less than you want, or just starting out, you can still use the Hourly Net Worth Formula by using your desired annual income. Think of the Hourly Net Worth you do want to have and use that amount. Then, watch as it grows into reality.

**GAGES**

Money is not the sole gage of effectively managing your time and activities. You can also think about your time in terms of how it benefits others. For instance:

- As a single mother living in Hawaii, I had to earn a certain income, so that I could afford to keep up with the cost of living and to provide for my daughter. It was crucial for me to have just one job because many Hawaii residents had to work at least two jobs to make ends meet. I wanted to make sure that I was able to leave work in time to pick up my daughter from school.

- Because I was only working one job, I was also eventually able to contribute my spare time to charities in my community, spend quality time with my daughter, and enjoy living a more balanced life.

## "I AM" STATEMENTS

At times, we can be our own biggest critics and worst enemies. Our minds can often make us believe very detrimental perceptions, which are called "limiting beliefs" and "negative thoughts." They can give us the feeling that we are frozen—unable to move forward with the vision we want to realize in our sales career.

Remember the Stuart Smalley skits on *Saturday Night Live*? You may have gotten a good laugh out of them. I certainly did, but the point of this sketch has substantial merit. See his famous daily affirmation:

### Daily Affirmation with Stuart Smalley

I am smart enough,

I am good enough,

And doggone it, people like me![20]

20 Al Franken, *I'm Good Enough, I'm Smart Enough, and Doggone It, People Like Me! Daily Affirmations By Stuart Smalley*, 1992

Stuart Smalley's character on *Saturday Night Live* was played by Al Franken, who is now a United States Senator for Minnesota. In 1992, Franken made a commitment to write daily affirmations for an entire year. Along with that commitment, he intended to compile those affirmations into a book and publish it.

Interestingly enough, Franken did not think that he was good enough or smart enough to be an author. His first affirmation he wrote in his book was about him being smart enough, good enough to be an author. Since releasing his first book, which contained all the affirmations he wrote daily for a year, he has written more than a dozen books. I would say that his affirmation of becoming an author worked!

In 2006, I completed a self-development seminar that encouraged me to use affirmations. Shortly after applying affirmations in my daily sales routine, I transformed my negative perceptions into empowering beliefs.

You've probably heard about the power of positive self-talk. "I Am" affirmations pinpoint this concept even more precisely. These statements get straight to the point without any fillers. When you say, "I am powerful," your subconscious mind embeds the feeling that you are powerful into that statement. If you say, feel, and believe it enough, you are bound to feel powerful.

Instead of calling these statements "affirmations," I prefer to call them "declarations." I believe that we already possess everything we need within ourselves. Instead of forcing them into our conscious and our being, we can use less energy by just drawing them out from within ourselves.

Since completing the seminar in 2006, I have been practicing what I call "The Declaration Ritual" by applying "I Am" statements to my daily sales training. This ritual is my secret sauce. It's the simplest exercise for self-development. It has helped me replace negative thoughts and unleash a powerful, creative side of me that remained hidden for too long.

Below are examples of the "I Am" statement I've used over the years:

- I am confident.
- I am empowering.
- I am creative.
- I am deserving.
- I am courageous.
- I am worthy.

**"I AM" EXERCISE**

Are there characteristics that you're concerned about not possessing? This exercise will help you start believing that you have these attributes by drawing them out of you. Then you will soon realize that you already embody those characteristics.

To experience the power of this exercise, follow these steps:

- Get colored 3x5 index cards and a black Sharpie.
- Write down one "I Am" statement on every card.
- Select qualities that you want, that you think you lack, or that you want to embody more often. You'll literally complete this phrase: I am ___. Write in the present tense and use adjectives.
- Display the cards in the parts of your home that you regularly visit. For example, put one on the bathroom mirror that you use every morning. Or pin one up on the wall in front of your desk. Post them all around the house, so that they become embedded in your subconscious wherever you go. Before you realized it, you won't even notice these 3x5 cards stuck on your walls throughout your house.
- Make sure that you display them at your eye level, or slightly above it. Looking up can lift your mood.
- Whenever you see them, absorb what they say. Take a moment to REALLY experience and feel that specific "I am." Use visualization and all your senses to truly believe it. For example, think of what the attribute of "confidence" looks, feels, and sounds like, and then embrace it.
- Say the words aloud, embrace the declaration, and live the statement. Tell yourself how good it sounds, and really see yourself being/having/doing that characteristic, quality, or state.
- Feel (or see in the mirror) how your posture changes to demonstrate your change in attitude, and feel (or see) your facial expression as you exhibit that attribute.

After you've incorporated "I Am" statements into your life, memorize this sequence and repeat it to yourself every time before you meet a new PC:

- *I watch my thoughts before they become my words.*
- *I watch my words before they become my actions.*
- *I watch my actions before they become my characteristics.*
- *I watch my characteristics before they become my reality.*

By using these "I" statements before meeting your PCs, you'll be buzzing with positive energy. When the PCs shake your hand, they will notice that your energy is different than any other sales representatives they've met. You will embody a "good energy" around you, which will get your sale presentations off on the right foot.

Before you meet any of your PCs, remind yourself of the following: You are going to have the opportunity to change your PCs' lives for the better—because owning your product/service will improve their lifestyles. Let go of the attachment on having this PC purchase from you. Instead, gear your intentions to be of service and bring value to them.

You deserve to have abundance in accordance to your Highest Values. Take great care of your mind, body, and spirit. Do activities that support your path to empowering you to apply the 60-Second Sales Method in every sales presentation. Use visualization as part of your daily habits. Be your own version of Stuart Smalley and create your list of declarations. You will be amazed by the sales career you create.

# CONCLUSION

## BELIEVE IT AND YOU WILL ACHIEVE IT

In preparing to write this book, I contemplated on the depth of knoweldge and experience that I would share with you. The intention of wanting you to thrive and learn how to earn your sales faster compelled me to let it all out in this book. I commend you for reading to this point. It took me 10 years, a total sum of $200,000 investment in my self-education, reading more than 200 books and articles, and facilitating over 2,000 sales presentations utilizing the 60-Second Sales Method for me to attain the techniques, methods, practices, and achievements that I've shared with you. Thank you for investing your time, funds, and energy in reading this book.

Take advantage of what is possible for you now in your sales career by studying, testing, and applying what you have learned. My intention was not to only save you time in your sales presentations, but to support you in having a more balanced life as well.

## CHECKLIST

Use this checklist to supplement your transformation to becoming a member of The Sales Elite. Each of the seemingly small components in the list below is a valuable piece of the puzzle. If you focus on well-being, joy, and gratitude in all aspects of your life, you are far more likely to achieve the success that you have been dreaming of in your sales career. If you're lacking one piece, the puzzle will never be complete.

- **A Gratitude Journal**
  Use a specific notebook for your daily journal, which will get you to cultivate an Attitude of Gratitude.

- **Exercise**
  Whether you choose to spend time in the gym or simply go for a walk outside, you need to exercise in order to obtain your peak performance. Movement allows your body to increase endorphins which will release stress and have you feeling like a champion.

- **Laughter**
  Since laughter is a natural way to enhance your mood, spend time watching your favorite sitcoms, funny movies, or standup comics. Spend time with people that cultivate your joy and humor. Avoid the doom room in your office and any drags on your positivity.

- **Wellness**
  Fuel your body with foods and beverages that will help it perform at its optimal level. Nourish your mind, not just your belly.

- **The Silver Lining**
  Optimism sustains your success. When you're challenged with a situation that's out of your control, ask yourself, "How does this serve me, the ones I love, or my clients?" In order for the Law of Attraction to work on your behalf you must be absolutely clear and focus on your intentions.

- **Focus**
  At work, avoid wasting time or energy on distractions, or anyone with a focus other than serving your PCs. The Circle of Appreciation generates powerful outcomes. Demonstrate your appreciation to your employer and PCs by staying focused on being of service.

- **Influence**
  Learn from those that have been where you are heading. Seek out mentors that will guide and encourage you. Invest your down time to read, watch movies or videos, or do other activities that truly inspire you. (See the "Recommended Reading" Appendices at the back of the book.)

- **Balance**
  To avoid burnout, focus on what you're great at (sales), delegate your other tasks, and automate as much as you can. Set your Daily Plan and Boundaries to ensure that you have scheduled free time to do as you please.

I use the following website services to delegate:

- Care.com (everything from dog walkers to assistants)
- Fiverr.com (starts a $5 for all sorts of online services)
- Guru.com (professional freelancers)
- Peopleperhour.com (professional freelancers)
- UberEats.com (delivers your food orders from restaurants)
- Upwork.com (professional freelancers)
- 99design.com (professional freelancers)
- Amazon.com (shop online for all sorts of items and groceries. Use a Prime membership for free deliveries.)

- **The Company You Keep**
  There is a common saying that "you are what you eat." I believe that we're also who we surround ourselves with.

  If you sell products, you regularly take an inventory. Now it's time to inventory your sales industry network. Avoid spending a majority of your work hours with coworkers that might not be in the right frame of mind to support your path to becoming a member of the Sales Elite. Instead, surround yourself with coworkers that believe in you and encourage your path to success.

## THE SALES ELITE

It is now time to truly start believing that you are on the path to becoming a member of the Sales Elite. When you follow the action steps and exercises detailed in this book, you will transform your sales career from the inside out. Your professional dealings will become more harmonious. You will achieve your sales goals with more ease and speed, and you will begin to amass wealth in ways that you never dreamed possible before.

We have all overcome massive challenges and obstacles in our lives. Personally, I had to quickly learn to speak English in order to communicate with my new family in a new country. For you, it might be dealing with a divorce, navigating financial setbacks, starting a new sales career, or relocating to a new, unfamiliar environment. These can all be challenging, difficult experiences, but when we leverage the fortitude and strength that we possess to overcome adversities in our careers and personal lives, we will both survive and thrive.

Live your best sales career; this is your time. Surround yourself with people who mentor and inspire you. Embody the things and people that you admire. Practice the proven sales process laid out in this book, which will lead you to a more fulfilled, sustainable sales career. Remember to treat your employer and PCs with respect and gratitude.

Right now, I want you to go back to the moment in time when you chose to pursue a career in sales.

Why did you choose this industry? Specifically, why did you begin your journey in sales? Was it the promise of abundance, the opportunity to make unlimited commissions, the thrill of enrolling the next client, or the drive of competition?

Now that you've remembered why you made this decision, it is important to ask yourself deeper questions. The questions salespeople ask themselves on a daily basis are what set apart those who are just surviving from those who are thriving. How many clients did you impact in a positive way? How have their lives and the lives of their loved ones been improved because you provided them with your product or service?

*You need to ask yourself these latter questions on a regular basis, since the answers will fuel your sales success. They need to be your constant reminders about why your Fair Exchange is a sustainable sales career.*

The Sales Elite enable people to enhance their lives with the products and services we offer them. We connect with individuals on a meaningful, respectful level and contribute to their livelihood. We may be selling a service that allows people to stay connected to their loved ones online, or selling homes that provide safety, security, and childhood memories. But the result is the same:

*When you embody the qualities of the Sales Elite, you become an integral part of the world, and provide products or services that contribute to people's Highest Values.*

Consumers need salespeople like you to assist them in getting what they want. As Zig Ziggler says: *"You will get all you want in life, if you help enough other people get what they want."* As I mentioned in the Introduction, it is no coincidence that you picked up this book out of thousands. And because you've completed reading it, then you are already on the path to becoming a member of The Sales Elite. Make the most of the 60-Second Sales Method and go breakthrough any ceilings that have held your sales production back. You now have the power, the tools, and sales method to make it happen.

# GLOSSARY

**6 Ws**    Key questions that start with the letter "W": What, Why, Who, When, Would, and Will.

**Analyst**    Personality type that goes with the flow, is formal, and relies on researching before making decisions.

**Anchoring**    Re-affirming the good feelings about memories and linking them to other experiences in a similar way.

**Brand Reliability**    The comfort created by product consistency.

**Caveat Emptor**    The idea that the buyer is accountable for her/his purchase.

**Caveat Venditor**    The idea that the seller is accountable for the product being sold.

**Choice Question**    Empowers a PC to choose from the options you present.

| | |
|---|---|
| **Circle of Gratitude** | A principle that involves gratitude among clients, employees, and employers. |
| **Clarifying Question** | Determines a PC's DBVs and reasons behind objections. |
| **Closed Question** | Evokes a simple "yes" or "no" answer from the PC. |
| **Conscious Mind** | Responsible for logic, thinking, and judgments. Handles non-complex decision making. |
| **Controller** | Personality type that is dominant, formal, and task-oriented. |
| **Customer Experience Movement** | The collective change of providing Superb Customer Experience. Going above and beyond potential clients and client's expecations. |
| **DBVs** | Dominant Buying Values. The focal point of the PC's HVs used to link the benefits of the product being sold. |
| **Directed Question** | Has a targeted focus on a certain subject area. |
| **Enrolling PCs** | Offering them something that improves their lives, as opposed to closing a sale. |
| **Fear of Loss** | Encourages PCs to feel that they'll miss out on an opportunity. |

| | |
|---|---|
| **Hope to Gain** | Feeds your PC's hope of gaining more than they currently have. |
| **Influential Question** | States a specific point of view in the form of a question. |
| **Mirroring** | A vital sales technique, which involves copying movements, verbiage, energy, and the emotions of your PCs. |
| **Monkey Brain** | A mind that is distracted. |
| **Negative Commands** | Instructions or directions that have a reverse effect, such as: don't think of the color red. |
| **Open Question** | Allows the person to share their values through their answers openly. |
| **Pacing/Leading** | Matching the tempo, body movements, expressions, or emotions of your PC, then setting the pace by leading. |
| **PCs** | Potential Clients. |
| **Present Listener** | Someone who is fully present, absorbing everything they hear without judgment. |
| **Promoter** | Personality type that is dominant, informal, and relationship-oriented. |
| **Rhetorical Question** | A statement in the form of a question. |

| | |
|---|---|
| **Sales Elite** | The top tier of salespeople, super-achievers, rank top 1%. |
| **Sensory Language** | Communicating through the senses (sight, sound, smell, taste, or touch). |
| **Subconscious Mind** | Processes up to 11,000,000 million bits of information per second. Stores long term memory and can handle complex decision making. Best used for the most complicated section of your sales presentation. |
| **Superb Customer Experience** | Sales presentations that are engaging and attentive for PCs, and help them get what they want. |
| **Supporter** | Personality type that goes with the flow and is informal and relationship-oriented. |
| **WVO** | Wyndham Vacation Ownership, largest vacation ownership company in the world. |

# SENSORY WORDS

## VISUAL/SEE

| | | | |
|---|---|---|---|
| See | Focus | Mark | Visualize |
| Gigantic | Perceive | Straight | Glance |
| Look | Shiny | Crooked | Open |
| Show | Observe | Foresee | Close |
| Tiny | Glimpse | Picture | Review |
| Watch | Notice | Clean | Clear |
| Obvious | Detect | Detect | Glance |
| Dull | Vibrant | Insight | Recognize |

## KINESTHETIC/TOUCH

| | | | |
|---|---|---|---|
| Touch | Hairy | Do | Own |
| Feel | Tension | Tend | Effect |
| Rough | Release | Action | Affection |
| Smooth | Handle | Crisp | Weak |
| Take | Experience | Move | Support |
| Pressure | Emotion | Express | Frigid |
| Sticky | Sensitive | Strong | Grasp |

## AUDITORY/HEAR

| | | | |
|---|---|---|---|
| Sound | Sizzle | Snappy | Loud |
| Say | Talk | Mention | Story |
| Tell | Discuss | Hum | Articulate |
| Hear | Hum | Squeak | Feedback |
| Buzz | Faint | Roar | Brassy |
| Share | Deafening | Crunch | Vocal |
| Noise | Hiss | Faint | Express |
| Shriek | Serene | Listen | Dialogue |

## GUSTATORY/TASTE

| | | | |
|---|---|---|---|
| Taste | Sweet | Stomach | Cheesy |
| Gut | Yummy | Bite | Swallow |
| Bland | Tangy | Bitter | Stink |
| Spicy | Zesty | Stale | Consume |
| Rotten | Bitter | Savor | Zest |
| Juicy | Bland | Sample | Gooey |
| Flavor | Sour | Drink | Season |
| Salt | Hungry | Cleanse | Buffet |

## OLFACTORY/SMELL

| | | | |
|---|---|---|---|
| Smell | Smoky | Acidic | Stuffy |
| Fishy | Rotten | Flowery | Aromatic |
| Fragrant | Earthy | Foul | Aroma |
| Pungent | Nasty | Fresh | Reek |
| Aroma | Burning | Musty | Burnt |
| Sweet | Medicinal | Funky | Odor |
| Old | Bouquet | Rancid | Whiff |
| New | Scent | Sharp | Sniff |

# RECOMMENDED READING

Bach, Richard. *Jonathan Livingston Seagull.*

Brady, Mark. The Wisdom of Listening.

Byrne, Rhonda. *The Secret.*

Dr. Demartini, John. *The Breakthrough Experience: A Revolutionary Approach to Personal Transformation.*

Dr. Demartini, John. *How To make One Hell of a Profit and Still Go to Heaven.*

Dr. Demartini, John. *Count Your Blessings: The Healing Power of Gratitude and Love.*

Duhigg, Charles. *The Power of Habit: Why We Do What We Do in Life and Business.*

Gay, Ben III. *The Closers Part 1 and Part 2.*

Godin, Seth. *The Purple Cow: Transform Your Business by Being Remarkable.*

Hawkings, R. David. M.D., Ph.D., *Power Vs. Force: The Hidden Determinants of Human Behavior.*

Hill, Napoleon. *Think and Grow Rich.*

Hogan, Kevin. *The Psychology of Persuasion: How to Persuade Others to Your Way of Thinking.*

Hogan, Kevin. *The Science of Influence: How to Get Anyone to Say "YES" in 8 Minutes or Less!*

Mandino, Og. *The Greatest Salesman in the World.*

Redfield, James. *The Celestine Prophecy: An Adventure.*

Sinek, Simon. *Leaders Eat Last: Why Some Teams Pull Together and Others Don't.*

Vaynerchuk, Gary. *Jab, Jab, Jab, Right Hook: How To Tell Your Story In A Noisy, Social Word.*

# ABOUT THE AUTHOR

A LINE BENDER WAS BORN in Vietnam and immigrated to France as a child, where she lived for 10 years. At the age of 11, Aline moved to the US to join her step-family. English as a Second Language classes were not offered in her new school in Houston, TX. She learned to speak, write, and communicate in English by watching the television show, *Sesame Street* and from studying in her school's library.

Her first sales job was selling beef jerky sticks door-to-door for her school's fundraiser. Aline fell in love with sales and continued her sales career in retail high-end sales for over a decade.

After going to college in California, she eventually found herself as a single mother of a toddler and living in one of the most expensive states in the country: Hawaii.

Most recently, Aline sold vacation ownerships at Wyndham Vacation Ownership for six years in Honolulu, HI. Throughout her sales career there, Aline ranked in the top 1% of Sales Representatives, broke sales records, and was promoted 5 times. She earned multiple awards: President's Club, President's Council, and Top Producer.

When she earned only $17,000 the year prior to her first job at Wyndham Vacation Ownership, she never thought that she'd earn $100,000 in just her first year selling vacation ownerships—and **half a million dollars** the year after that!

It took hard work, discipline, investment in her self-education and self-development, and an unwavering drive to succeed and grow. But most of all, it required applying the 60-Seconds Sales Method.

Aline is now co-owner of Kamai'ana Mortgage Group Inc., and a sales trainer. She is happily married and resides in San Diego, CA with her husband, daughter, and husky mix. She is a volunteer at the Junior League of San Diego and is on the council of Training & Development.

To learn more about Aline, visit her site at:
**www.alinebender.com**